Mentoring with Meaning

Previous Titles

Mentoring

The Effects and Effectiveness of Mentoring in Education

Mentoring with Meaning

*How Educators Can Be
More Professional and Effective*

Edited by Carlos R. McCray
and Bruce S. Cooper

ROWMAN & LITTLEFIELD
Lanham • Boulder • New York • London

Published by Rowman & Littlefield
A wholly owned subsidiary of The Rowman & Littlefield Publishing Group, Inc.
4501 Forbes Boulevard, Suite 200, Lanham, Maryland 20706
www.rowman.com

Unit A, Whitacre Mews, 26-34 Stannary Street, London SE11 4AB

Copyright © 2015 by Carlos R. McCray and Bruce S. Cooper

All rights reserved. No part of this book may be reproduced in any form or by any electronic or mechanical means, including information storage and retrieval systems, without written permission from the publisher, except by a reviewer who may quote passages in a review.

British Library Cataloguing in Publication Information Available

Library of Congress Cataloging-in-Publication Data

Mentoring with meaning : how educators can be more professional and effective / edited by Carlos R. McCray and Bruce S. Cooper.
pages cm
Includes bibliographical references and index.
ISBN 978-1-4758-1796-6 (cloth : alk. paper) -- ISBN 978-1-4758-1797-3 (pbk.) -- ISBN 978-1-4758-1798-0 (electronic)
1. Mentoring in education. I. McCray, Carlos R. II. Cooper, Bruce S.
LB1731.4.M474 2015
371.102--dc23
2015016540

∞ ™ The paper used in this publication meets the minimum requirements of American National Standard for Information Sciences Permanence of Paper for Printed Library Materials, ANSI/NISO Z39.48-1992.

Printed in the United States of America

Contents

Preface   vii
   Bruce S. Cooper and Jan Hammond

1   What Is Mentoring? What Does It Mean?   1
   Heather Wynne, Ken Cuthbert, and Carlos R. McCray

2   Mentoring in a Global Society: Academic Mentoring of International Students   13
   Kathleen P. King, Julie Leos, and Lu Norstrand

3   How Leaders Mentor Others to Be Leaders . . . Or Don't   35
   Michael R. Mascellino

4   Catholic School Mentoring for Mission and Ministry   49
   Mary Ann Jacobs

5   Meaning-Making Mentoring through Communication, Relationships, and Caring in Higher Education   69
   Floyd D. Beachum

6   Peer Mentoring, Coaching, and Collaboration: New Strategies for School Reform   85
   Karen Andronico

7	Leadership Practices in Mentoring *Richard Savior*	113
8	Instant Mentoring: The Promises and Perils of E-mentoring *Rhonda S. Bondie*	129
9	Preparing Women to Lead: Relating Mentoring to Success *Deirdre Callahan*	149

Index	165
About the Contributors	175

Preface

Bruce S. Cooper and Jan Hammond

This book, *Mentoring with Meaning,* and its forthcoming companion, *Making Mentoring Work,* should help educators to mentor or to be mentored effectively in our schools. We all have had mentors—those key adults from family, work, or schools—who have assisted us in learning and becoming good adults, skilled and able professionals, and contributing members of community and society. Although it's not easy, it does occur and is doable, and this book seeks to help everyone—educators in particular—both to be mentored and to be a mentor.

In fact, we believe and show that everyone needs mentoring and many have the capacity, knowledge, and savvy to be helpful mentors to others in their field, school, and world. We have reduced the process to five word sets, represented by the acronym *M.A.R.C.H.*, meaning the following:

>M—Modeling with Meaning
>A—Advancement through Advisement
>R—Review and Revise
>C—Coping and Copying
>H—Hope and Help

THE MARCH TO MENTORING

Modeling with Meaning

We all have and are modeling ourselves after colleagues, friends, and family who can assist and have assisted us in life, and we can imitate and use their ideas, spirit, and knowledge to our own benefit. After all, jobs like teaching are highly personal and interpersonal; they model and express what we believe and do in the classroom, schools, and elsewhere. And we all remember what some *models* have done and said while teaching us that affected us positively, profoundly, and deeply.

I'll never forget what Professor Donald A. Erickson, PhD, did for me at the University of Chicago one day. Based on Dr. Erickson's recommendation and help, I was able to complete and publish a study for Richard Nixon's President's Commission on School Finance. I was thus given an opportunity to gather data and publish a report for the Commission entitled *Free and Freedom Schools: A National Survey* (1971). I presented the findings to the Commission, headed by Neil H. McElroy, president of Proctor & Gamble, which were published in a report and sent to libraries across the country.

When I met later with Dr. Erickson to thank him personally and give him a printed, published copy of my Commission report, he excused himself, went downstairs to the dean's office, and returned with the Master of Art (MA) degree paperwork for me to fill out and for us to sign. I thus received training, support, caring, funding, and yes, mentoring—and an MA degree for my work on the Commission Report. And I shall never forget what this effort meant and means to me: a degree, a national publication, and a chance to investigate "alternative" schools some forty-three years ago. And I participated in a living model of mentoring that I have often used with my students in their doctoral program efforts: *mentoring in action with meaning.*

Advancement through Advisement

Mentoring often helps newcomers to teach and school leadership to learn their trade—skills, techniques, language, and behavior—to become quality professionals. Thus, one must see mentoring not as a single act, but as a life-long effort and process of giving and learning, taking and *advancing*, which never stops. Having mentored over two hundred students to their doctorate before retiring, I can tell much about the process of mentoring, a career-long process. One advises and assists colleagues and students in writing, publishing, teaching, leadership, and mentoring; and I tried often to help my students to publish their dissertations as books and/or articles, and I helped them advance their careers and skills.

Review and Revise

Mentoring is not always easy or perfect; and mentors must be both critical and helpful, if mentees are to grow and learn their jobs as teachers, scholars, administrators, and the like. When I submitted my report to the President's Commission and knew it would be widely read, I worked extra hard to fulfill my responsibilities to the field, the schools, the university, and Presidential Commission. One must always imagine what the readers and users of one's work will learn and do and work toward helping them advance toward these goals.

Reviewing leads often to *revising*, and rewriting, to get it right. Mentoring is thus a cooperative effort between the mentor and the mentee—and both learn and grow with the interactions and experiences. This book gives multiple examples of just how mentors act and how mentees respond; it's definitely a two-way street and process, running "both ways."

Coping and Copying

Mentees often have chances to model their behavior after their mentor-teacher, learning to take a field, ideas, and requirements and gear them to their students by both focusing the students' attention and inspiring them to listen, learn, and practice what they see in the classroom. And leaders, too, *cope* and *copy* with and by their leadership styles that are both inspirational and commanding. Thus, mentees cope by copying, and their mentors model and reinforce the lessons and techniques. It's a daily, ongoing, and critical process.

Hope and Help

We see that the end result often is the ability and willingness of leaders to help and to share hope with their followers. Thus, the MARCH to mentoring is long and critical if new teachers are to learn from the senior instructors; and leaders can inspire their followers and fellow leaders. One can see and sense the process, and we spell them out in these two new books, step-by-step, method-by-method, and outcome-by-outcome.

Each chapter takes a different stance, but all can inspire and teach us to be both good and better at our jobs. Jan Hammond and Rita Senor's great book, *The Mentor: Leading with Heart* (1971), reminds us, "And, yes, it is each leader's job to mentor the next generation of leaders who make this a better world in which to live" [and go to school].

REFERENCES

Cooper, Bruce S. (1971). *Free and freedom schools: A national survey of alternative programs.* Washington, DC: President's Commission on School Finance.

Hammond, Jan, & Senor, Rita (1971). *The mentor: Leading with heart. The ultimate resource.* New York: iPublisher.

Chapter One

What Is Mentoring? What Does It Mean?

Heather Wynne, Ken Cuthbert, and Carlos R. McCray

As a newcomer, it is normal to feel overwhelmed and unsure of how one integrates within one's professional community. It is common to seek out and find guidance and support from others who have been in the field or system. Mentoring is a major component of one's career development (Fowler, 1982) and a service to the community at large (NFIE: National Foundation for the Improvement of Education, 1999). Mentoring relationships have positive, long-lasting effects on both the individuals involved and the professional community.

Throughout the process, both the mentor and mentee change and grow in the field and within themselves. Traditionally defined as a more seasoned professional guiding a less experienced individual, the term *mentoring* has gone through further development. As research and exploration into this process have expanded, so has its understanding and conceptual framework.

Much value and utility emerge in the mentoring process. In Tareef's (2013) study with faculty members from the University of

Jordan, most faculty members indicated that their career had been influenced by at least one person, with mentoring descriptions ranging from advisory partnerships to more traditional mentoring and modeling. Meta-analyses of research articles suggest that mentoring has a positive impact on increasing commitment to the organization, enhancing job satisfaction, and fostering a feeling of self-esteem (Underhill, 2006).

Mentoring—specifically for one's career—is usually related to promotions and higher salaries (Allen, Eby, Poteet, Lentz, & Lima, 2004). Although decreasing work stress was also an outcome of mentoring relationships, the effect size was minor (Underhill, 2006). Mentor characteristics such as gender, age, number of years of experience in the professional workplace, and type of career often affected the degree of impact from mentoring (Eby, Durley, Evans, & Ragins, 2006). How professionals perceived their mentoring experience as beneficial and supportive also influenced their willingness to mentor in the future (Eby et al., 2006).

Overall, value and utility occur in seeking out mentors as a newcomer and to eventually becoming a mentor later on in one's life. This chapter will describe how the mentoring construct has developed over the decades, important approaches to mentoring, and applications to leadership. It is our hope that these two textbooks will be a resource to guide everyone through their early career years and evolve into a source of insight and reflection as one's career path becomes solidified with experience and expertise.

HISTORY OF MENTORING IN RESEARCH LITERATURE

Mentoring was first conceptualized in ancient Greek methodology when Odysseus trusted a man named Mentor to take care of his son when going to war (Merriam, 1983; Allen & Eby, 2010). Levinson is often cited (Allen & Eby, 2010; Garvey et al., 2008) as the first author to initiate the study of mentoring, specifically through his book *Seasons of a Man's Life* (Levinson, Darrow, Klein, Levinson, & McKee, 1978). Levinson conducted a longitudinal study on males in mentoring relationships across forty years and explained mentoring as a developmental process. It wasn't until Kram's (1985) book, *Mentoring at Work: Developmental Relationships in Organizational Life*—regarding mentoring functions and relationships—that the field truly flourished in research and popularity (Allen & Eby, 2010).

At this juncture, mentoring was traditionally defined as experienced professionals in the field educating younger professionals just starting their careers (Kram, 1985; Levinson et al., 1978). Kram (1985) more explicitly defined mentoring along with its functions such as including career and psychosocial support (Allen et al., 2004). Thus, concrete benefits of mentoring regarding career objectives, as well as the interpersonal and social-emotional support of a more experienced professional educating newcomers—have been introduced in literature since the inception of the mentor construct.

Mentoring is a dynamic, parallel process, where the mentor and mentee both learn and grow as professionals in their careers while helping each other. The mentoring process has been under much review and research throughout the past few decades. Haggard, Dougherty, Turban, and Wilbanks (2011) analyzed about forty definitions of *mentor* over time throughout research literature. Specifying a concrete definition of the mentoring process is difficult as individuals perceive their mentors, and/or the process in itself, differently (Kram, 1985; Haggard et al., 2011). The differentiation of *formal* mentoring surfaced in the early 2000s to distinguish this framework from *informal* mentoring, which deviates from the traditional concept of an older, more seasoned veteran guiding a less experienced protégé (Haggard et al., 2011).

Overall, the terms *protégé* and *mentee* are used when individuals acknowledge that they have a mentor, which is different from receiving *mentoring functions* (e.g., counseling, sponsorship, visibility, and confirmation; see Haggard et al., 2011). Upon analyzing mentoring articles dating back to 1980, Haggard et al. (2011) suggested three aspects of mentoring, which are "reciprocity, developmental benefits, and regular/consistent interaction over some period of time" (p. 292). It is not our focus to constrict the terms of *mentor* and *mentoring*; we ask that you examine the limitless possibilities of seeking out mentors in your workplace, who may be different from your supervisors.

APPROACHES TO MENTORING

Since mentoring involves the collaboration and relationship of both the mentor and mentee (Ghosh & Reio, 2013), identifying approaches that align with an individual's career success is important. Mentoring is a parallel process, where either the mentor or protégé can influence and guide the outcomes of the relationship. Reciprocity is needed in this parallel process, where the mentor can benefit interpersonally (Shore, Toyokawa, & Anderson, 2008), as the protégé is learning and growing in the field. To create a successful mentoring relationship, the mentor and protégé's expectations, interpersonal styles, and personalities should align and complement each other. A newcomer should seek an experienced professional who would allow for professional growth but also look for an optimum match.

Developmental Processes

Above all else, a developmental process is critical to the mentoring relationship. Kram (1983) highlighted four phases to mentoring: initiation, cultivation, separation, and redefinition. Either the mentor or mentee may initiate or start the mentor relationship that will cultivate or grow over time. Before beginning to form a relationship, the mentees should reflect and assess what their strengths and weaknesses are, as well as their goals and focus toward the mentoring relationship (Mullen & Schunk, 2012). Without a purpose, the mentoring process may lack direction and simply stop.

However, changes may occur to distance the two individuals, where the relationship may end or refocus. Separation may occur when the mentee has learned all the skills necessary to function independently, or when the individuals involved no longer wish to be in the relationship (Mullen & Schunk, 2012). When the mentor and protégé wish to continue the connection, the mentoring may become redefined into a more balanced, supportive relationship (Mullen & Schunk, 2012).

Mentoring will be different with a protégé's being completely new to the field versus a colleague switching organizations within the same career. In the first case, mentors may teach their protégés required skills and information for their career. When a mentee is more seasoned in the field, the mentor may give insight into the organization or helpful tips to assist protégés with their careers. Both the stages and contexts of mentoring are important to identify and reassess throughout the relationship. As a newcomer, you may wish to seek help in sophisticating your skills, or feel the need for more independence.

Relationships among Mentors and Protégés

More importantly, the relationship between the mentor and mentee is of significant importance. Attachment theory (Bowlby, 1973; Ainsworth, 1991) has been connected to studying the effectiveness of mentoring relationships (Wang, Noe, Wang, & Greenberger, 2009). Bowlby's (1973) original research focused on the mother-child dyad and how people may develop their personal schemas of their environment from their relationship experience. Ainsworth (1991) expanded upon this notion and asserted that individuals can more adequately explore their environment when they hold a secure and close relationship with someone.

Wang et al. (2009) conducted a study to assess whether the time spent in mentoring and the mentoring attachment styles in low and high extremes of anxiety and/or avoidance (e.g., secure, preoccupied, dismissing, fearful) impacted the protégés' desire to mentor in the future. Overall, mentors and protégés in a secure relationship, as noted by low avoidance and low anxiety, reported more willingness to mentor in the future than mentors and protégés reporting high levels of anxious relationship styles (Wang et al., 2009).

Thus, interpersonal and relationship styles may bolster or negatively impact one's career goals and the mentoring process. A mentor must also acknowledge potential barriers to success. Some challenges may arise from gender differences, lack of honesty, and a need for power and autonomy (Barret et al., 2009). Although the mentoring relationship does not need to be *intimate* or socially close (Haggard et al., 2011), it is important that both the mentor and mentee have similar needs with regard to their desired level of closeness and collaboration. As in any relationship, the mentor and mentee's interpersonal styles and attachments should also meet each other's expectations.

Effective Mentoring Qualities

Many effective and beneficial skills and qualities of good mentors transcend mentoring across professionals. Expanding off of Kram's (1985) mentor functions, empathy in a mentor predicted psychosocial aspects of mentoring, and helpfulness predicted increased levels of career mentoring (Allen, 2003). NFIE (1999) identified four sets of characteristics of good mentors, specifically regarding their attitude/character, communication skills, interpersonal skills, and professional competence/experience. The successful mentor must also realize the basic components needed from the mentee for the mentoring process to be effective: understanding of leadership and teaching, solid communication skills, openness, and commitment to the mentoring process (Daresh & Playco, 1994).

Contemporary Approaches to Mentoring

As educational and occupational approaches change with society, so may the way in which we see the mentoring relationship. For example, due to the increasing demand for technology, mentoring does not need to be held in the traditional person-to-person context within the same workplace. *Electronic mentoring* (Haggard et al., 2011) can occur through electronic communication, such as Google chat, video, and through online discussion boards.

The collaborative mentoring model (Mullen, 2000) highlights how professionals in different areas can work together to construct a shared outcome. Examples include partnerships between practitioners and researchers, where both can benefit from the process (Mullen, 2000). Other models of mentoring include peer and co-mentoring, where the relationship is more balanced in respect to expertise (Garvey, Stokes, & Tegginson, 2008; Underhill, 2006). Further, school leaders reported how nontraditional mentors who helped, supported, or taught them to be successful at their workplace were an integral part of their career success (Mendez-Morse, 2004). Thus, as you the newcomer are developing what professional areas you would like mentoring in, you should also assess what type of mentoring you would prefer to seek.

LEADERSHIP APPLICATIONS TO MENTORING

We hope by now that everyone is aware of the concept of mentoring, independent of supervisors or role models, and see the value and utility of seeking out a mentor. As discussed above, protégés and mentors hold multiple connections and can cultivate various relationships. In the field of education, school superintendents oversee and are responsible for the overall operation and well-being of the school district(s) under their charge.

Being accountable for such magnitude of responsibility, some consider these individuals to be the equivalent of private industry's chief executive officers. Given their wide range of responsibility, it would be in the best interest of those new to the position and to the school district(s) under their charge that new superintendents receive support and mentoring that would bolster their chances for being successful. After all, studies have found that leaders who have formal or informal mentors tend to have better job performance (Alston, 1999).

Consistent with Kram's (1985) delineation of career and psychosocial mentoring, mentors often communicate and connect on an emotional level with their mentees, while assisting them in the physical, emotional, and logistical aspects of school leadership (Allen, Jacobson, & Lomotey, 1995). Given the multitude of studies highlighting the utility and value of mentoring, it is safe to assert that mentors can make a positive difference in the career lives of their protégés. The type of relationship a protégé holds with a mentor is important, as well as the presence of a mentor relationship. Having a mentor can increase an individual's chances of securing a position (Moody, 1983). Protégés may have preferential treatment by their social network and through mentors' recommendations (Moody, 1983). Thus, seeking a mentor may help you in the immediate future in your workplace, as well as in future endeavors requiring networking and collaboration.

Finding a mentor in an organization may prove difficult for various reasons. Given that demographics such as gender, age, number of years in the professional workplace, and career types impact the amount of mentoring in organizations (Eby et al., 2006), we may not have the opportunity to have a mentor readily at hand. Some educational leaders have succeeded without the benefits provided through traditional mentoring relationships, as indicated in Kowalski and Brunner (2011). As a protégé, if you feel isolated or unable to seek mentorship, it is possible to construct and seek pathways to pursuing your personal and professional goals (Kowalski & Brunner, 2011).

If we cannot seek mentoring in the traditional sense in our professions, we can explore nontraditional mentoring approaches such as online professional networking associations, colleagues in similar positions, and outside companies or school systems. With the advent of media use and technology, it is possible to have a beneficial mentoring partnership with individuals outside of our geographical area. Expanding our social and professional network will only benefit our professional career.

CONCLUDING STATEMENTS

The mentoring process goes through stages in development and should not be static in nature. The mentor and protégé or mentee should constantly redevelop the relationship to maximize the benefits to both parties. Moving from being defined as an older member educating a less experienced professional (Kram, 1985; Levinson et al., 1978), the term *mentoring* has expanded to include reciprocity among individuals, developmental benefits in the organization, and consistent communication over a period of time (Haggard et al., 2011). A mentor does not simply support or provide guidance, but holds an open, supportive relationship that should be cohesive with a protégé's interpersonal style and expectations.

So, what happens now? As a newcomer, you should first start out with expectations you have for yourself and how you want to grow as a professional. A match between your styles and needs to a mentor is just as important as the expertise or experience level of the mentor. Keeping in mind barriers to mentoring, you may have to navigate your professional organization for a couple of weeks to seek out a prime mentoring relationship.

When we are in a mentoring relationship, it is always beneficial to continuously grow and reciprocate the support to our mentor. This way, the mentoring relationship can become redefined as we-progress through our career. We will be on our way to becoming leaders in our organizations as we continuously allow and seek growth opportunities, both personally and professionally.

REFERENCES

Ainsworth, M. S. (1991). Attachments and other affectional bonds across the life cycle. In C. M. Parkes, J. Stevenson-Hinde, & P. Marris (Eds.), *Attachment across the life cycle* (pp. 33–51). London & New York: Routledge.

Allen, K., Jacobson, S. & Lomotey, K. (1995). African-American women in educational administration: The importance of mentors and sponsors. *Journal of Negro Education, 64*, 409–422.

Allen, T. (2003). Mentoring others: A dispositional and motivational approach. *Journal of Vocational Behavior, 62*, 134–154. doi: 10.1016/S0001-8791(02)00046-5

Allen, T., & Eby, L. (2010). *The Blackwell handbook of mentoring: A multiple perspectives approach*. West Sussex, UK: John Wiley & Sons Ltd.

Allen, T., Eby, L., Poteet, M., Lentz, E., & Lima, L. (2004). Career benefits associated with mentoring for protégés: A meta-analysis. *Journal of Applied Psychology, 89*, 127–136. doi: 10.1037/0021-9010.89.1.127

Alston, J. (1999). Climbing hills and mountains: Black females making it to the superintendency. In C. C. Brunner (Ed.), *Sacred dreams: Women in the superintendency* (pp. 79–80). Albany, NY: New York Press.

Barret, T., Girardot, K., Chevers, I., Kundu, R., Savage, S., & Evan, L. (2009). A conversation about mentoring. *Visual Art Research, 35*, 1–10.

Bowlby, J. (1973). *Attachment and loss: Vol. 2. Separation*. New York: Basic Books.

Daresh, J. C., & Playco, M. (April 1995). Mentoring in educational leadership development: What are the responsibilities of the protégé? Paper presented at the annual meeting of the American Educational Research Association (AERA), San Francisco, CA.

Eby, L. T., Durley, J. R., Evans, S. C., & Ragins, B. R. (2006). The relationship between short-term mentoring benefits and long-term mentor outcomes. *Journal of Vocational Behavior, 69*, 424–444. doi: 10.1016/j.jvb.2006.05.003

Fowler, D. L. (1982). Mentoring relationships and the perceived quality of the academic work environment. *Journal of the National Association for Women Deans, Administrators & Counselors, 45*, 27–33.

Garvey, R., Stokes, P., & Megginson, D. (2009). *Coaching and mentoring: Theory and Practice*. Thousand Oaks, CA: Sage Publications.

Ghosh, R., & Reio, T. G. (2013). Career benefits associated with mentoring for mentors: A meta-analysis. *Journal of Vocational Behavior, 83*, 106-116. doi: 10.1016/j.jvb.2013.03.011

Haggard, D. L., Dougherty, T. W., Turban, D. B., & Wilbanks, J. E. (2011). Who is a mentor? A review of evolving definitions and implications for research. *Journal of Management, 37*, 280–304. doi: 10.1177/0149206310386227

Kowalski, T. J., & Brunner, C. C. (2011). The school superintendent: Roles, challenges, and issues. In F. English (Ed.), *Handbook of educational leadership: Advances in theory, research, and practice* (pp. 109–133). Thousand Oaks, CA: Sage Publications.

Kram, K. E. (1983). Phases of the mentor relationship. *Academy of Management Journal, 26*, 608–625. doi: 10.2307/255910

———. (1985). *Mentoring at work: Developmental relationships in organizational life.* Glenview, IL: Scott, Foresman.

Levinson, D. J., Darrow, C. N., Klein, E. B., Levinson, M. H., & McKee, B. (1978). *The seasons of a man's life.* New York: Knopf.

Mendez-Morse, S. (2004). Constructing mentors: Latina educational leaders' role models and mentors. *Educational Administration Quarterly, 40*, 561–590. doi: 10:1177/0013161X04267112

Merriam, S. (1983). Mentors and protégés: A critical review of the literature. *Adult Education Quarterly, 33*, 161–173.

Moody, G. (1983). On becoming a superintendent: Contest or sponsored mobility. *Journal of Negro Education, 52*, 383–397.

Mullen, C. A. (2000). Constructing co-mentoring partnerships: Walkways we must travel. *Theory into Practice, 39*, 4–11. doi: 10.1207/s15430421tip3901_2

Mullen, C. A., & Schunk, D. H. (2012). Operationalizing Phases of Mentoring Relationships. In S. Fletcher & C. Mullen Eds., *SAGE Handbook of Mentoring and Coaching in Education.* Thousand Oaks, CA: Sage Publications.

National Foundation for the Improvement of Education (NFIE; 1999). *Establishing high-quality professional development.* Washington, DC: NFIE.

Shore, W. J., Toyokawa, T., & Anderson, D. D. (2008). Context-specific effects on reciprocity in mentoring relationships: Ethical implications. *Mentoring & Tutoring: Partnership in Learning, 16*, 17–29. doi: 10.1080/13611260701800926

Tareef, A. B. (2013). The relationship between mentoring and career development of higher education faculty members. *College Student Journal, 47*, 703–710.

Turban, D. B., & Lee, F. K. (2007). The role of personality in mentoring relationships. In Belle R. Ragins & K. Kram (Eds.), *The handbook of mentoring at work* (pp. 23–35). Thousand Oaks, CA: Sage Publications.

Underhill, C. M. (2006). The effectiveness of mentoring programs in corporate settings: A meta-analytical review of the literature. *Journal of Vocational Behavior, 68*, 292–307 doi: 10.1016/j.jvb.2005.05.003

Wang, S., Noe, R. A., Wang, Z. M., & Greenberger, D. B. (2009). What affects willingness to mentor in the future? An investigation of attachment styles and mentoring experiences. *Journal of Vocational Behavior, 74*, 245–256. doi: 10.1016/jvb

Chapter Two

Mentoring in a Global Society

Academic Mentoring of International Students

Kathleen P. King, Julie Leos, and Lu Norstrand

INTRODUCTION

In the twenty-first century, our global society has created a different community of students within U.S. higher education institutions (Institute of International Education, 2012). Rather than being dominated by U.S. residents and "sprinkled" with international students, universities, colleges, and programs court students from abroad as prime tuition paying prospects (Ferdman, 2014). Therefore, our classrooms have greater numbers of international students, which full-time and part-time faculty must learn to teach simultaneously and successfully.

In addition to the challenges of successfully teaching international students in undergraduate courses of different sizes, there is the challenge of mentoring them at the graduate and doctoral levels. Building upon a foundation of adult learning principles and research, this chapter presents the need for a model of mentoring international graduate and doctoral students in the United States within the context of our twenty-first-century global society. The model synthesizes several adult learning theories, the mentoring literature, and research about international graduate students.

THE NEED

The numbers of international students in U.S. colleges and universities have risen sharply in the last five years due to many factors. As of 2012, students studying in the United States from foreign nations numbered 800,000. It is expected this number will continue to rise because U.S. institutions rely increasingly on the differential of foreign tuition to provide significant portions of their budgets (Ferdman, 2014).

Our businesses and society demand different outcomes among college graduates today. They must be prepared to utilize critical thinking, organizational insight, lifelong learning, and self-directed learning (SDL) skills in problem solving and leadership contexts (King & Cox, 2010). Such higher-order thinking, deftness of skill, and application are in stark contrast to the expectations of prior decades for employees to perform rote tasks or strictly standardized protocols. In these ways, higher education's mix of student communities, expected achievements, and job placements are more complex than ever before.

This section briefly introduces the need for a mentoring model to serve international graduate and doctoral students through scenarios and the literature. While the scope of need is great, the variety of needs is infinite due to the diversity of human experience.

UPSIDE DOWN IS NOT A TYPE OF CAKE

Munir was a Palestinian international student in the United States. He was enrolled in an educational research program in a university in the Southwest. He and his family had consulted several people and agencies about his study in the United States. Topics discussed included climate differences, cultural habits, dietary concerns, availability of mosques for his religious observance, and visa, passport, and immunization requirements. However, the most difficult adjustment was not discussed: the differences in academic performance expectations.

When Munir received his first paper back from the professor, he was surprised at the failing grade. The comments kept referring to "critical thinking" and analysis. What was she asking him to do? When he met with the professor he found out that the educational expectations of Palestinian and U.S. professors were entirely different. While his professors at home valued memorizing entire books, the American professors wanted him to analyze them and ask questions about meaning and alternatives. He was lost.

All his life he had been rewarded for repeating the entire book verbatim: the more exactly identical, the better! Now, his entire world was upside down. They don't want the truth at all! They want the students to create their own words! How could this be university education?

He went to the mosque that weekend and talked to some students there. They were American students and could not understand the confusion and frustration he described passionately. He returned to campus with no answers. Tuesday he visited his advisor, hoping to drop the course, and probably college. It was Dr. Advance who revealed the cause of his frustration. She said that the two countries had very different educational approaches, even philosophies, and it was based on their history: His country had a strong oral tradition of memorization, while

> the United States taught critical analysis as the preferred approach even in the younger grades. She offered peer tutoring for him with an advanced international Asian student. He could work with Munir to help him learn the differences and the expectations for assignments.

Mentoring becomes a powerful means to differentiate the learning experience of professionals who will ultimately work in different contexts. While whole group instruction may address macro scope issues of content, higher-order thinking, and globalization, mentoring may be leveraged to cultivate specific insights for international students' successful placement and transition into the professional world. While many international students might initially express the desire to return to their country once they complete their studies, recent reports indicate that 50 percent stay for at least an extra year (Ferdman, 2014). Based on their areas of study, the demand for international students' expertise is strong in the U.S. job market as well: 50 percent of U.S. students major in STEM, business, or marketing compared to greater than 67 percent of foreign students (Ferdman, 2014).

When we reach beyond undergraduate education, the waters of competing demands become even more torrential. Our international graduate and doctoral students have the needs described above, but also must prepare for professional placement in a foreign culture. This confluence becomes the crux of mentoring international students in higher education based on the needs of a global society and the twenty-first century. Faculty, who have received little or no preparation in how to design or evaluate teaching and learning, must also grapple with complex interactions among foreign cultures, multiple languages, rapidly increasing knowledge bases, and instantaneous information exchange.

This chapter proposes a mentoring model to inform faculty and those responsible for professional development. The model is grounded in the literature of adult learning theories and practices, international student needs, and mentoring. It provides a comprehensive view mentoring international graduate and doctoral students in the twenty-first century.

INTERNATIONAL STUDENT NEEDS

The overall enrollment of international graduate students increased 7 percent in 2012–2013 (International Students Enrollment, 2014). The challenges encountered by international students in the United States have been well documented. Language, social and cultural differences, and communication may hinder international students from getting involved in campus activities and discourage them from interacting with other students (Dee & Henkin, 1999; Ryan et al., 1998; Zhai, 2002). Stress resulting from these challenges puts international students at great risk for academic difficulties (Poyrazli & Kavanaugh, 2006) as well as psychological problems (Mori, 2000).

This section introduces the needs of international students in U.S. colleges and universities as identified in the literature. Based on a review of the literature, two areas of focus were identified: what the institutions perceived the international students' needs were, and what the students recognized them to be.

Institutional Perspective

U.S. institutions have operated numerous programs to address the needs of international students (Dee & Henkin, 1999; Filice, 2010). Many universities assign an American student as a peer leader in the orientation; however, these orientations are provided before the semester begins and the primary purpose is to allow the new and international students to become familiar with the campus (Filice, 2010). Advisors can help students choose a major, schedule their coursework, and answer their academic queries (Filice, 2010).

However, evidence shows that the influence of these institutional programs may be limited. Poor participation in orientation sessions and peer support programs show that institutional efforts may not completely meet the needs of international students (Merta, Ponterotto, & Brown, 1992). Furthermore, counseling services are underutilized by most students (Pedersen, 1991).

Although many institutions advise students who want to study abroad to have a language school course (Jiang, 2005), about one third of international students rate their own performance upon arrival as inadequate, and an even higher number of students lack adequate proficiency skills in English (Huntley, 1993). Although they practice speaking and listening to English, they usually speak their own language (Jiang, 2005). Educators of American higher education should be aware of the inequality of English proficiency between international students and American students (Hsieh, 2007). Particularly, the academic mentoring that includes emotional and psychological support, role modeling, and career guidance may be more significant for international graduate students because they are also dealing with language barriers (Ku et al., 2008).

Student Perspective

As far back as 1993, Huntley recognized that the number of international graduate students equals and was likely to surpass the number of international undergraduate students. The complex situation that international graduate students face can be conceptualized as being in a "double liminal" between the home and host cultures (Jeeseon, Kaori, & Tamiko, 2012). Although they may have obtained a formal education background and a good working knowledge of the language of the host country, they likely need to adjust socially and emotionally to gain an advanced degree and enhance their employment opportunities (Dee & Henkin, 1999; Huntley, 1993). Ku et al.'s (2008) research finds that institutions need to continue to address academic support mechanisms for international doctoral students. Specifically, they recognize that "mentoring has been beneficial particularly for doctoral students of color seeking careers in academia" (p. 366).

Research by Myles and Cheng (2003) demonstrates that social support and adjustment are major issues for most international students as they go abroad and study without their family and friends. Therefore, they need to build new social circles and social networks that are completely different from the connections fostered in their home country. Their qualitative research included interviewing twelve nonnative English-speaking international graduate students (Myles & Cheng, 2003). The findings revealed that international students tended to associate primarily with people from their own culture for many purposes, including social life. Ku et al. (2008) support these findings in their recommendation that institutions and individuals who mentor international graduate and doctoral students consider ways to build their connections and network with others of diverse customs.

Furthermore, while international graduate students have demonstrated consistently higher indicators of quality than their American colleagues, their different cultural backgrounds may bring additional challenges for them (Huntley, 1993). The cultural gap may cause a high level of anxiety and uncertainty (Yuan, 2011), which can lead to maladjustment and failed communication (Gudykunst, 2005).

Continuing this theme of support needs, research by Kaczmarek et al. (1994) reveals that international students appear to experience difficulty seeking support when needed. Olivas and Li (2006) delineate the following influences on facilitating cultural awareness and sensitivity by both international and domestic U.S. students: Positive relationships among international students and faculty, the perceived high quality of instruction, and faculty interest in students' professional development are all critical to organizational and personal success.

THEORETICAL FOUNDATIONS

In building a theoretical foundation for an international model of graduate mentoring, and based on our prior work, reading and experience in the area, we recognized three major areas to include: SDL, transformative learning (TL), and mentoring models. This section presents those findings from the literature that were most relevant to the needs of international graduate and doctoral students.

SDL and TL are both within the field of adult education that originated from teaching in workplace settings (Lindeman, 1926). Adult learning is characterized by principles of learner-centeredness, immediate application, student respect, and cultivating lifelong learning strategies, all of which assist professionals in successfully navigating changing environments and demands (Knowles, 1975; Merriam & Bierma, 2013). In stark contrast to traditional teacher-centered undergraduate education, the adult learning orientation of mentoring moves the learner to the "driver's seat" of their current and future professional development. Indeed, adult learning principles are at the core of twenty-first-century learning, such as critical thinking and intercultural competencies (King & Cox, 2010; Merriam, Caffarella, & Baumgartner, 2006; Han & Henschke, 2012; Henschke, 2009).

Self-Directed Learning

Knowles (1975) posed the characteristics of SDL. Later, others, including Brockett and Hiemstra (1991), advanced the theoretical framework and applications to different settings, including higher education (Candy, 1991; Silen & Uhlin, 2008). The premise of SDL is to identify the steps through which adults identify learning needs, resources, and strategies independent of an instructor (Wang & Cranton, 2012). Further understanding has also developed to illuminate the differences between the processes and content of SDL. This perspective created more understanding of how to support people in reaching mastery of SDL in a variety of ways.

In 1981, Mezirow's efforts to delineate a critical theory of adult learning and education delineated twelve core concepts to facilitate adults developing as self-directed learners. Suanmali (1981) tested Mezirow's core concepts of SDL; his research resulted in confirming eight of these strategies for cultivating SDL skills among adult learners.

The confirmed concepts that cultivated SDL include the following eight steps: (1) decrease learner dependency, (2) help learners use learning resources, (3) assist learners to define their learning needs, (4) encourage learners to take responsibility for learning, (5) foster learner decision-making and choices, (6) support learner judgment and integration, (7) facilitate problem-posing and problem solving, and (8) provide a supportive learning climate.

Transformative Learning

Much as self-directed learning emerged from the core concepts of adult learning, so did TL. In fact, Mezirow was still advancing the SDL theory in 1981 when he wrote the first research report about transformative learning (1978). TL is a powerful model that includes an approach for mentoring international graduate and doctoral students because it explains how adults may successfully cope with difficult life dilemmas and reach new understandings of themselves and others (Cranton, 1994, 2006; King, 2005, 2009a, 2009b; Mezirow, 1978, 1991).

The development of TL has been driven by both theoretical discussion and research (Cranton, 2006; King, 2005, 2009b; Mezirow & Associates, 2000; Taylor & Cranton, 2014). Several schools of thought have evolved since its origin in 1978. The one applied in our model is holistic and considers the entire life of learners in how they navigate difficult choices, complex dilemmas, and synthesis of new perspectives (Cranton, 2006; King, 2005, 2009b).

TL models have varying numbers of stages depending on which research or theorist one reads. However, many of them agree that TL includes adult learners navigating four to twelve stages—although not necessarily in a single order (see King, 2005, 2009b; Mezirow & Associates, 2000; Snyder, 2008; Taylor & Cranton, 2014). The model includes the following five steps and qualities: (1) encountering a "disorienting dilemma" (Mezirow, 1978); (2) critically examining beliefs, values, and/or assumptions; (3) testing new ways of thinking; (4) adopting new perspectives, habits of mind, or worldviews; and (5) taking action based on this new understanding and perspective.

The power of TL for understanding the needs and means to support professional success among international graduate and doctoral students rests in several characteristics (Stevens-Long, Schapiro, & McClintock, 2012). TL provides the following:

1. An open-ended timeline for adults to navigate through disorienting changes, which reflect the wide variety of circumstances and personalities among students (King, 2005, 2009b).
2. Learners and faculty building a complex, yet comprehensible, framework for making sense of the many confusing experiences encountered (for instance, cross-cultural communication, foreign practices of critical thinking, clashing cultural practices, unusual spiritual experiences, etc.) (King 2009b; Snyder, 2008; Taylor, 2008; Taylor & Cranton, 2012).
3. A holistic frame for authentic professional choices (i.e., it includes culture, emotions, intellect, etc.) (King, 2009b; Snyder, 2008; Taylor & Cranton, 2012).
4. Strategies for incorporating critical thinking and synthesis of new understandings (Mezirow & Associates, 2000; Stevens-Long et al., 2012; Snyder, 2008; Taylor, 2008).
5. Means to develop solutions for complex cultural and professional situations, including, for example, the following process: as learners internalize TL strategies, they may deftly, even unconsciously, navigate multidimensional conflicts (King, 2009b; Mezirow & Associates, 2000).

Mentoring in Graduate and Doctoral Studies

During and following graduate education, students usually are assigned a "mentor" (with some title or another) to guide them through their research work. As identified in the research, mentees indicated key characteristics of a mentoring relationship that included both "exchanging knowledge" and providing role modeling (Eller et al., 2014). When one considers that graduate and doctoral students are in the midst of transitioning from more than eighteen to twenty-three years of formal education (from kindergarten to their master's) and on to independent professional life, they encounter not only major academic hurdles to surmount, but also entirely new challenges in their chosen profession. The literature on mentoring in academia and its counterparts (e.g., coaching in business settings) are complementary in revealing similar needs for guidance and support (King, 2009a).

What does the term *mentor* mean? Many people choose a definition that includes "one who guides less experienced colleagues through the novice stages of their profession." In some cases, people have more than one mentor to address different aspects of their career. For instance, a junior faculty member may seek mentors for doing research, publishing, teaching, and grant writing.

Professional advancement is not composed of simplistic skill sets or strategies; therefore, having multiple experts as mentors (e.g., in teaching, grant getting, writing, publishing, and present work and ideas) can be a wise choice. The nature of a mentorship includes the ability for mentors to help mentees increase their academic and/or workplace performances (Daloz, 1988). Eby et al. suggest a "significant [relationship] between workplace mentoring and career attitudes, work attitudes, and some career outcomes" (2008, p. 263).

A research study by Chao, Walz, and Gardner (2006) reveals that mentored individuals scored higher in their ability to manage the politics, people, and goals of an organization than nonmentored individuals. Nakamura and Shernoff (2009), in their book *Good Mentoring*, discuss the benefits of mentoring relationships as they are often influential in the construction of professional values and the capacity for a mentee to understand and practice distinctive professional principles and philosophies. More importantly, mentees "begin to define the kind of professional they want to become" (Nakamura & Shernoff, 2009, p. 3).

In a research study conducted by Anderson and Anderson (2012), domestic doctoral students identified the overall benefit of having a mentor when they indicated that having a faculty mentor was "considered a significant advantage" (p. 242). Having someone guide them through the research and publication process was very important for them. Their mentors also helped them by providing "insight into faculty roles, [and] professional capital to help compete for faculty positions" (p. 247). Those students without mentors stated they were not "prepared for any faculty roles at similar institutions" (p. 247).

It is widely recognized that formal education can induce stress on adult learners (Daloz, 1988). In the case of international doctoral students, the additional element of cultural differences often created added pressure and strain (Ku et al., 2008). Furthermore, not having someone to direct international students to understand cultural and political implications of their new roles could further detach students from overall success.

According to a study conducted by Ku et al. (2008) regarding international doctoral students in a mentoring support group, students desired the opportunity to learn about gaining professional positions, researching and publications, cultural adjustment, and making social connections. Furthermore, the study showed the ultimate desire of international doctoral students to feel cared about. Advisors and mentors could do this by "being available, working with the students, and showing extra patience" (Ku et al., 2008, p. 375).

In the context of academia, knowledge of nuanced cultural differences and practices is essential for successful transition. Ideals such as proper expectations and ethical standards are more helpfully gained through mentor guidance than from real-life mistakes. Furthermore, Ku et al. (2008) discuss the differing viewpoints that international students possess regarding their knowledge (or lack thereof) of the difference between being a researcher and being a faculty member.

International doctoral students have the desire to understand potential job roles and what it means to be a faculty member in the United States (Han & Henschke, 2012). Because of students' status as novices, they often do not grasp what they do not know. Thus, prioritizing the mentorship of international graduate and doctoral students should be in the forefront in planning for their entering into a profession.

A Mentoring Model

More structured support systems are needed to ensure the success of the large number of international students enrolled in U.S. higher education. In considering the above discussion, we constructed a model (see figure 2.1) that synthesizes and represents the theoretical foundation of the proposed mentoring model for international graduate and doctoral students. This figure illustrates how the essential theoretical bases converge to create a conceptual framework of mentoring.

Figure 2.1 graphically represents our theoretical framework. In order to effectively mentor international graduate and doctoral students in the United States, faculty benefit from incorporating

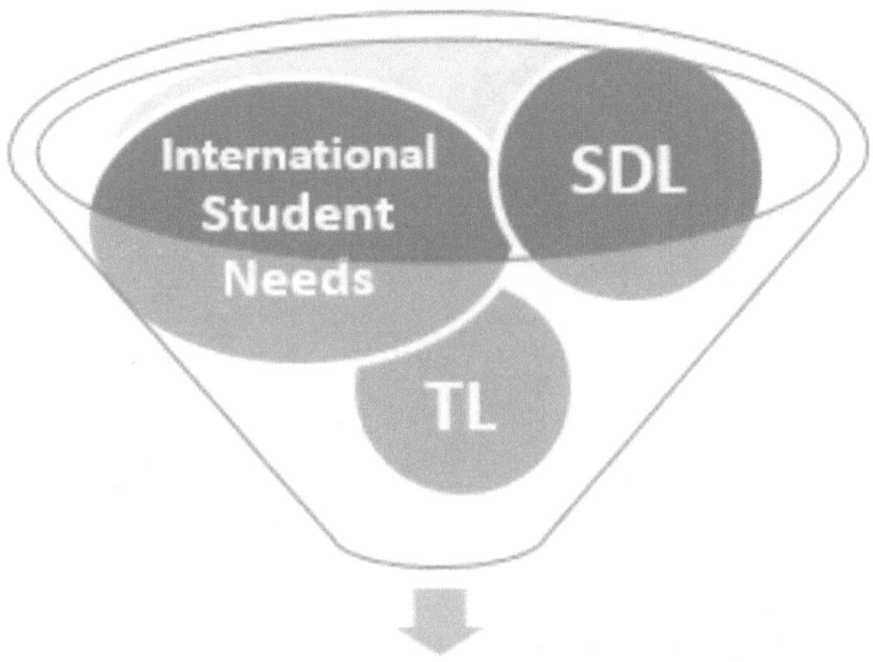

Figure 2.1. A Theoretical Framework of Mentoring Model for International Graduate and Doctoral Students (Authors' note: The relative scale of each "theory" is not representative, only necessary for design purposes.)

understanding international student needs, SDL theory and practices, and TL concepts. In contrast to this theoretical construct, we wanted to also illustrate the relationship of these theories to the *practice* of mentoring. These efforts resulted in the design in figure 2.2.

In our experience, and that of others as well, faculty have prime opportunities to support student-centered perspectives and strategies while mentoring graduate and doctoral students (Bauer, 1985; Hansman, 2008; Ibrahim, 2002). Why? Among many reasons, at this point, learners realize the expansiveness and complexity of knowledge. Consequently, they also confront that they cannot learn

Figure 2.2. A Practical Framework of Mentoring Model for International Graduate and Doctoral Students

everything they need to know for the future from their formal education. This stage of development creates a readiness to discover how to continue to learn beyond university and without their instructors within reach. These realizations provide powerful motivation for mastering SDL strategies prior to entering and during their professional careers.

As stated previously, the literature documents that doctoral studies for international learners have the potential not only to create stress (Poyrazli & Kavanaugh, 2006) but also transformational learning experiences (Taylor, 2008; Taylor & Cranton, 2012). The proposed model leverages the best practices identified in research and theory thorough a grounded research model of practice.

Moreover, this mentoring model aligns with a transition model that Schlossberg (2011) maintains students must successfully navigate. Her model has been widely studied and cited in the field of student and academic affairs. Four Ss represent Schlossberg's transition model: (1) situation, (2) self, (3) supports, and (4) strategies (2011, p. 160). The proposed practical model addresses a specific "situation" affecting international graduate and doctoral students in the United States. The theoretical foundation (figure 2.1 above) includes theory and the model (figure 2.2) incorporates SDL strategies to address the second S, self.

Positive mentors easily qualify as support because they can truly "help the person getting through the transition" (Sargent & Schlossberg, 1988, p. 60). Additionally, the focus of the practical model includes "strategies" for coping and success that are specific to the needs and interests of this population. This proposed model synthesizes the literature and provides theoretical and practical guidance for faculty and institutions to address the needs of international graduate and doctoral students in the United States.

CONCLUSION

This chapter presents a grounded model in the research and related literature to provide two interdisciplinary models for mentoring international graduate and doctoral students in the United States. The models include not only institutional programs but also faculty mentoring, which provide support in building independently successful professionals.

The objectives of these models include achieving success rather than just program graduation. They incorporate development of SDL skills and TL coping strategies in international graduate and doctoral students' mentoring. In addition, the models provide a framework for cultivating the development of professionals with multidimensional worldviews and the strategies to successfully navigate them.

REFERENCES

Anderson, S., & Anderson, B. (2012). Preparation and socialization of the education professoriate. *International Journal of Teaching and Learning in Higher Education, 24*(2), 239–251.

Bauer, B. A. (1985). Self-directed learning in a graduate adult education program. *New Directions for Continuing Education* (25), 41–49.

Brockett, R. G., & Hiemstra, R. (1991). *Self-direction in adult learning: Perspectives on theory, research, and practice.* New York: Routledge.

Candy, P. (1991). *Self-direction for lifelong learning.* San Francisco, CA: Jossey-Bass.

Chao, G. T., Walz, P., & Gardner, P. D. (2006). Formal and informal mentorships: A comparison on mentoring functions and contrast with nonmentored counterparts. *Personnel Psychology, 45*(3), 619–636.

Cranton, P. (1994). *Understanding and promoting transformative learning.* San Francisco, CA: Jossey-Bass.

———. (2006). *Understanding and promoting transformative learning: A guide for educators of adults.* San Francisco, CA: Jossey-Bass.

Daloz, L. (1988). *Mentor: Guiding the journey of adult learners.* San Francisco, CA: Jossey-Bass.

Dee, J. R., & Henkin, A. B. (1999). Challenges to adjustment to college life in the United States: Experiences of Korean students. *International Education, 29*(1), 54–70.

Eby, L., Allen, T. D., Hoffman, B. J., Baranik, L. E., Sauer, J. B., Baldwin, S., & Evans, S. C. (2008). An interdisciplinary meta-analysis of the potential antecedents, correlates, and consequences of protégé perceptions of mentoring. *Psychological Bulletin, 139*(2), 441–476.

Eller, L. S., Lev, E. L., & Feurer, A. (2014). Key components of an effective mentoring relationship: A qualitative study. *Nurse Education Today, 34*, 815–820.

Ferdman, R. (2014, August 29). Where foreign students are from. *The Washington Post.* Retrieved from http://www.washingtonpost.com/blogs/wonkblog/wp/2014/08/29/where-foreign-students-are-coming-from/

Filice, K. (2010, March 29). *International students and American university life*. Retrieved from http://www.hurriyetdailynews.com/n.php?n=american-university-life-nowadays-offers-an-increased-global-awareness-2010-03-29

Gudykunst, W. B. (2005). An anxiety/uncertainty management (AUM) theory of strangers' intercultural adjustment. In Williams B. Gudykunst (Ed.), *Theorizing about intercultural communication* (pp. 419–457). Thousand Oaks, CA: Sage.

Han, P., & Henschke, J. A. (2012). Cross-cultural learning and mentoring: Autoethnographical narrative inquiry with Dr. Malcolm Shepherd Knowles. *International Journal of Adult Vocational Education and Technology (IJAVET), 3*(3), 26–36. doi:10.4018/javet.2012070103

Hansman, C. A. (2008). Context of adult learning. *New Directions for Adult & Continuing Education* (89), 43–52.

Henschke, J. A. (2009). "The beginnings of the history and philosophy of andragogy 1883–2000." In V. Wang (Ed.), *Integrating adult learning and technology for effective education* (pp. 1–30). Hershey, PA: IGI Global.

Hsieh, M. (2007). Challenges for international students in higher education: One student's narrated story of invisibility and struggle. *College Student Journal, 41*(2), 379–391.

Huntley, H. (1993). Adult international students: Problems of adjustment. *ERIC Document, 355,* 886.

Ibrahim, D. Z. B. D. (2002). Manifestation of self-directed learning by adult students in a post-graduate distance education program. School of Graduate Studies, University Putra Malaysia. Doctoral dissertation. Retrieved from http://psasir.upm.edu.my/9282/1/FPP_2002_9_A.pdf

Institute of International Education. (2012). *Top 25 places of origin of international students, 2010/11–2011/12*. Retrieved from http://www.iie.org/opendoors

Jeeseon, P., Kaori, W., & Tamiko, M. (2012). Culturally sensitive mentoring for Asian international students in counseling psychology. *Counseling Psychologist, 40*(6), 895–915.

Jiang, S. (2005, December 06). *Problems of international students*. Retrieved from http://soojinjang.blogspot.com/2005/12/problems-of-international-students.html

Kaczmarek, J., Castellani, P., Nicolo, G., Spina, B., Allemanni, G., & Zaridi, L. (1994). Distribution of oncoferal fibronectin isoforms in normal, hyperplastic and neoplacstic human breast tissues. *International Journal of Cancer, 58,* 11–16.

King, K. P. (2005). *Bringing transformative learning to life*. Malabar, FL: Krieger.

———. (2009a). Coaching—Mentoring: A different perspective. In M. Miller and K. P. King (Eds.), *Empowering women through literacy* (pp. 147–156) Charlotte, NC: Information Age Publishing.

———. (2009b). *Handbook of evolving research approaches in transformative learning: The Learning Activities Survey (10th Anniv. Ed.).* Charlotte, NC: Information Age Publishing.

King, K. P., & Cox, T. (Eds.). (2010). *The professor's guide to taming technology: Leveraging digital media, Web 2.0 and more for learning.* Charlotte, NC: Information Age Publishing.

Knowles, M. S. (1975). *Self-directed learning: A guide for learners and teachers.* Englewood Cliffs, NJ: Prentice Hall/Cambridge.

Ku, H. K., Lahman M. K., Yeh, H-T., & Cheng, Y. C. (2008). Into the academy: Preparing and mentoring international doctoral students. *Education Technology Research & Development, 56,* 365–377.

Lindeman, E. C. (1926). Andragogik: The method of teaching adults. *Workers' Education, 4,* 38.

Merriam, S., & Bierma, L. (2013). *Adult learning.* San Francisco, CA: Jossey-Bass.

Merriam, S., Caffarella, R., & Baumgartner, L. (2006). *Learning in adulthood: A comprehensive guide.* San Francisco, CA: Jossey-Bass.

Merta, R. J., Ponterotto, J. G., & Brown, R. D. (1992). Comparing the effectiveness of two directive styles in academic counseling of foreign students. *Journal of Counseling Psychology, 39,* 214–218.

Mezirow, J., & Associates. (2000). *Learning as transformation: Critical perspectives on a theory in progress.* San Francisco, CA: Jossey-Bass.

Mezirow, J. (1978). *Education for perspective transformation: Women's re-entry programs in community colleges.* New York: Teacher's College, Columbia University.

———. (1991). *Transformative dimensions of adult learning.* San Francisco, CA: Jossey- Bass.

———. (1981). A critical theory of adult learning and education. *Adult Education, 32*(1), 3–27. doi:10.1177/074171368103200101

Mori, S. (2000). Addressing the mental health concerns of international students. *Journal of Counseling and Development, 78,* 137–144.

Myles, J., & Cheng, L. (2003). The social and cultural life of non-native English speaking international graduate students at a Canadian university. *Journal of English for Academic Purposes, 2,* 247–263.

Nakamura, J., & Shernoff, D. J. (2009). *Good mentoring: Fostering excellent practice in higher education.* San Francisco, CA: Jossey-Bass.

Olivas, M., & Li, C. (2006). Understanding stressors of international students in higher education, *Journal of Instructional Psychology, 33*(3), 217–222.

Pedersen, P. (1991). Counseling international students. *The Counseling Psychologist, 19,* 10–58.

Poyrazli, S., & Kavanaugh, P. (2006). Marital status, ethnicity, academic achievement, and adjustment strains: The case of graduate international students. *College Student Journal, 40*(4), 767–780.

Ryan, D., Markowski, K., Ura, D., & Liu-Chiang, C. Y. (1998). International nursing education: Challenges and strategies for success. *Journal of Professional Nursing, 14*(2), 69–77.

Sargent, A., G., & Schlossberg, N. K. (1988). Managing adult transitions. *Training and Development Journal, 42*(12), 58–60.

Schlossberg, N. K. (2011). The challenge of change: The transition model and its applications. *Journal of Employment Counseling, 48*(4), 159–162.

Silen, C., & Uhlin, L. (2008, August) Self-directed learning: A learning issue for students and faculty! *Teaching in Higher Education, 13*(4), 461–475.

Snyder, C. (2008). Grabbing hold of a moving target. *Journal of Transformative Education, 6*(3), 159.

Stevens-Long, J., Schapiro, S., & McClintock, C. (2012). Passionate scholars: Transformative learning in doctoral education. *Adult Education Quarterly, 62*(2), 180–198.

Suanmali, C. (1981). *The core concepts of andragogy.* (Order No. 8207343, Columbia University Teachers College). *ProQuest Dissertations and Theses.* Retrieved from http://search.proquest.com/docview/303122821?accountid=14745.

Taylor, J. (2008). Fostering transformative learning and self-directed learning: Searching for connections. *International Journal of Self-Directed Learning, 5*(2), 23–34.

Taylor, E., & Cranton, P. (Eds.). (2012). *The handbook of transformative learning: Theory, research, and practice.* San Francisco, CA: Jossey-Bass.

Wang, V. C., & Cranton, P. (2012). Promoting and implementing self-directed learning (SDL), *International Journal of Adult Vocational Education and Technology (IJAVET), 3*(3), 16–25.

Yuan, W. (2011). Academic and cultural experiences of Chinese students at an American university: A qualitative study. *Intercultural Communication Studies, 1,* 141–157.

Zhai, L. (2002). *Studying international students: Adjustment issues and social support.* San Diego Community College District, Unpublished manuscript.

Chapter Three

How Leaders Mentor Others to Be Leaders ... Or Don't

Michael R. Mascellino

A competent mentor is a necessity as select teachers begin to pursue aspirations of becoming department or school leaders. However, more often than not, aspiring school leaders encounter disconnected, jealous, and generally poor mentors who have managed to secure a position and may be poor models of good leadership. Thus, the better-trained and more competent upcoming leaders encounter difficulty becoming established because the "old guard" is refusing to let go of its power and start sharing their competencies with the newcomers to the field.

Mentoring is an essential component in developing future school leaders. Not only is past experience shared, but it also provides opportunity for staff members to be gradually introduced to a new role and perspective. This experience essentially provides unspoken approval during the changing of the guard. In addition, mentoring is an essential component for not only the new leader to learn, but also for the entire organization (i.e., including classrooms, schools, and districts).

Students, staff, parents, and local municipalities make it their business to have a vested interest in their school leaders. They want to know that new leaders are knowledgeable, competent, and, above all, good listeners and leaders. As a school evolves, so do the people within it. Senge (1990) explained this delicate process:

> We become able to re-create ourselves. This applies to both individuals and organizations. Thus, for a learning organization it is not enough to survive. "Survival learning" or what is more often termed "adaptive learning" is important—indeed it is necessary. But for a learning organization, "adaptive learning" must be joined by "generative learning," learning that enhances our capacity to create. (p. 14)

According to Fullan (2007), leadership is complex because it entails a plethora of demands and expectations that must personally be met and be continually modified. As Fullan states,

> Commitment to *what should be changed* often varies inversely with knowledge about *how to work through a process of change*. The adage, "Where there's a will, there's a way," is not always the most effective way to think of mentoring because there are plenty of choices, and can get in the way rather than navigate a mentee in the right direction. . . .
>
> Clarity and a precise set of objectives and goals create a great set of guided visions; but those very visions without analysis and understanding the abilities of a mentee result in impatience, failure to listen, and disregard for flexibility. (2007, pp. 108–109)

However, despite the stress associated with the position, principals can be successful, according to Fullan's list of the criteria of successful principals, when they have the following: (1) "inclusive, facilitative orientation"; (2) "institutional focus on student learning"; (3) "efficient management"; and (4) "combined pressure and support" (Fullan, 2007, pp. 108–109).

The criteria mentioned above lay the foundation for dealing with the incoherence within the system and keep a focus on maintaining a functioning school, while making changes at the same time. Effective educational leaders stimulate their environment by infusing harmony with high standards and developing an "experiential" approach to improving the school and/or solving problems. Fullan (2007) describes how teachers and schools need to be recognized as "moral change agents" making democratic communities possible. Fullan also believes this endeavor is "worth fighting for" and over time can improve schools.

The next question is, how do new school leaders gain the necessary skills and knowledge that are required not only to survive but also to flourish during their early years? It becomes essential that the existing leadership must gradually introduce the new leaders to the school's daily routines and responsibilities to be effective at their new job.

However, let's take this one step further: where do many school leaders receive their training? In 2001 a survey was conducted of ninety-eight principals, of whom forty-four were interviewed to identify the learning process of new school leaders/administrators. The results indicated that many principals-in-training learn their responsibilities through continuous relevant on-the-job training (Brown, Anfara, Hartman, Mahar, & Mills, 2001).

Several individuals from the Brown, Anfara, Hartman, Mahar, and Mills (2001) study further requested, if not recommended, that all new principals should have collegial support in some fashion, including networking with other school leaders to exchange, if not evaluate, the demands that a new school leader will experience during that first year. On-the-job training serves well if the individuals walking into the school have background knowledge.

Moreover, transitioning textbook understandings of leadership and applications of it in the real world are two very different things. However, very few school districts have new-leader mentorship programs for learning. It's one thing to provide mentors during the graduate school years, where the learning still takes place in a vacuum/protected oversight of a professor. What happens after graduate school, especially if newly graduated school candidates don't receive a position immediately? One cannot ignore that new school leaders have "practical knowledge" of their job duties, learned from what they studied and interned for. However, each school district is different, with its own specific challenges and needs.

School leaders are under observation not only from their peers, but also by parents and the student population. All individuals seek the guidance and experience of the school leader when times are both good and bad. As I recall, I was given an article, "Being the Boss is Hard" (Ginsberg, 2008), which described the emotional and mental challenges that school leaders face. Such topics vary with the pressures of making tough decisions, bringing order out of chaos, whether to follow one's heart, and if moving forward with a particular plan will be beneficial or backfire.

After reading that, I came to a very concise conclusion: future leaders must be confident in themselves and learn gradually how to harness multiple leadership abilities so as to manage effectively all challenges (emotional, cognitive, etc.) that will be faced. This task is not easy, especially for those seeking a strong and capable mentor. School leaders are expected to perform a particular role; thus stress and emotional conflict are part of the profession.

Furthermore, in my experience, leaders are complex individuals, where their minds are constantly thinking, making decisions, formulating, and confronting difficult issues that cannot be easily resolved. Being a school leader means being placed in a tough position. Transforming cultures is the most difficult and challenging profession; and principals are overloaded with responsibilities that hinder developing and practicing these new competencies.

One must come to the understanding that both school leadership and the process of mentoring leaders are a complex business, as no one knows for sure what is best, in a world where decisions and consequences go hand-in-hand. Notwithstanding such complexities, "preparation guidelines" for states and school districts should be designed to maintain accountability and ensure high quality mentoring and assessment for new leaders.

Reasons for Poor Mentoring

The Wallace Foundation (2007) questioned why so many states and school districts are behind in developing "quality mentoring" programs. Their research indicated that the traditional "buddy system approach," with "check-list" requirements, is nothing more than a "to-do" list with little about "how to do" or "not do." Many of the common indicators of such loosely constructed programs consist of the following:

- Vague or unclear goals
- Insufficient focus on instructional leadership and/or overemphasis on managerial role
- Weak or nonexistent training for mentors

- Insufficient mentoring time or duration to provide enough sustained support to prepare new school leaders for their multifaceted job challenges
- Lack of meaningful data to assess benefits or build a credible case for sustained support
- Underfunding and lack of support

In addition, many stakeholders in the public feel that principal mentoring does not exhibit immediate or transparent results to school and student successes. Whereas with teachers, the results are more readily seen since students spend nine-tenths of their day with their teachers (The Wallace Foundation, 2007, p. 5) and students are regularly tested. One must also bear in mind that at the present time, no state or district guidelines exist for selecting mentors, training them, appropriate criteria for matching with mentees, financial compensation for mentors (incentives), and assessment or mentors, if they provided adequate levels of leadership development (The Wallace Foundation, 2007, p. 5).

A Successful Mentoring Program

With the above comments mentioned, Crocker and Harris (2002) conducted research from mentors and mentees in a school leadership/principal preparation program to allocate data in identifying necessary components of a successful mentoring program. The research suggested that the following should be done:

- Provide mentors with extra time to spend with their mentee, perhaps by releasing the mentor from other duties.
- Make specific guidelines available to mentors outlining meaningful activities and ways to involve mentees in these experiences.

- Require mentors to participate in formal training that emphasizes relationship building and professional collaborative behaviors (Crocker & Harris, 2002).

Successful mentoring programs must also be designed with experiences that best serve the mentees, where upon graduation they have authoritative approval of successfully demonstrating and mastering of the competencies necessary for improving student learning (SREB, 2007, p. 27). Capasso and Daresh (2001) state:

> These internship experiences should be designed to be meaningful and highly professional learning experiences. They should be meant to provide for a long-term evaluation of a student's leadership ability in a school setting by those practicing professionals who are most experienced in those settings. (2001, p. 26)

When responsibilities are clearly defined during the internship, it allows for key district and university stakeholders to perform their assigned tasks effectively and with a level of confidence. In addition, it holds staff members accountable for providing a high-quality internship experience for their mentees (SREB, 2007, p. 25).

Components in Being a Productive Leader and Competent Mentor

If any of the following interrelated components are missing or deficient, then the school leader must reassess his/her situation before embarking on any new ideas, policies, and even their methodology of mentoring. In addition, school leaders are expected to create more leaders—that is, to mentor!—in addition to building teams, being data-driven decision makers, and being inspirational (Fullan, 2007, p. 167). This is not an easy task; but over time, it can be done through careful preparation of ideas and methodologies, through proactive mentoring, and through scaffolding new school leaders to be efficient, dedicated, and competent. Fullan also explains that educational leadership is a complex business and no one really knows for sure what is best. In addition, Fullan says that successful leaders must engage in the following to meet the demands of their profession (including mentoring new leaders) and be prepared for the complexity it brings:

1. Setting directions (shared vision and group goals, high performance expectations)
2. Developing people and roles (individual support, intellectual/emotional stimulation, modeling)
3. Redesigning the organization (collaborative cultures and structures, building productive relations with parents and the community) (Fullan, 2007, p. 166).

Principals' Behavior and Professional Conduct

Principals must not only handle the day-to-day demands of the school, but also identify and implement new policies and ideas that could make their school run more efficiently and provide more opportunities for their students. This can only be accomplished once the school's capacity has been identified. Such prerequisites include *teachers' knowledge, skills, and dispositions*, which entails professional development, where the information must be connected to collective learning. Another is *professional community,* which means that the individuals as a group have responsibility and stake in increasing school capacity. Moreover, *program coherence* describes how programs are developed for student and staff learning. These programs must be coordinated and focused and identify clear-cut goals that can endure. In addition, *technical resources* must be taken into account, which includes space, expertise of trained personnel, time, equipment, and material. Lastly, *principal leadership*, where the mission of any administrative leader is about enhancing knowledge and skills within the organization and at the same time creating a common cohesive culture that has clear expectations for those with the special skills and knowledge in various parts of the organization. This contributes to the establishment of productive relationships and accountability for those involved (Fullan, 2007, p. 164).

Preparation Now

The question beckons, why aren't school leader programs assigned viable mentors for better preparing our future principals? If one were to really disseminate the data and see the daily responsibilities of school principals, it becomes obvious that having a solid, dedicated mentor, someone truly vested in the success of their mentee, we would see a tremendous improvement in school efficiency and leadership integrity.

The present "sink-or-swim" mindset that mentors have towards their mentees is obsolete and utterly absurd. How can any new school leader learn and be productive if the cards are already stacked against them? This type of situation makes new leaders look deficient and completely undermines their ability to be successful. Unqualified or lackluster mentors may employ this tactic to keep competition out.

Regarding actions needed by states, universities, and districts, the following should include several paramount components. First, university leadership—where preparation programs, partnerships with their public school districts, and joint responsibility and measurable levels of accountability towards their mentees and mentors—must be created to ensure that each side is benefiting. In addition, district and university leaders must meet to define school improvement plans and challenges. Moreover, internship criteria must include problem-based learning experiences. Lastly, mentoring standards should be established for mentees and mentors—including specific criteria for selecting qualified mentors and matching them with suitable mentees (SREB, 2007, p. 31).

Does Mentoring Have a Place in the Future?

Without formalized programs designed to train and evaluate mentors, an immense teacher and leadership vacuum exists, where existing school leaders with malicious intentions can undermine a new leader's ability to succeed and thwart the entire learning process. Moreover, the lack of data makes measuring mentoring's efficacy difficult, if not impossible.

Presently, for too many school leadership preparation programs, the internship "ship" is unsound, rudderless, or still in dry dock (SREB, 2005, p. 3). Many programs lack purposeful "hands-on" experiences that would prepare aspiring school leaders to develop the essential work of school improvement and higher student achievement *prior to being placed at the helm of a school* (SREB, 2005, p. 3). As Lovely (2004) states:

> To better align school district needs with principal preparatory programs, partnerships need to be established between a university and a single district or a consortium of districts. The goal of any partnership is to provide more meaningful learning experiences and flexibility to students. (Lovely, 2004, p. 23)

The concept of "shared responsibility" or "distributed leadership" has been a tough sell between universities and school districts, in part, because each side desires to have complete creative control over governance of school leadership programs.

In essence, the academic and school community has no idea how well or poorly new school leaders are be trained. In addition, it brings to question the quality and expertise of mentors. Students are evaluated by the NJASK (New Jersey Assessment of Skills and Knowledge), STAR (Standardized Test for the Assessment of Reading), GEPA (Grade Eight Proficiency Assessment), and, soon, PARCC (Partnership for Assessment of Readiness for College and Careers). Teachers are evaluated by SGOs (Student Growth Objectives), SGPs (Student Growth Percentiles), Common Core, and their principals to ensure "quality twenty-first-century education." We test our students and teachers to the point of exhaustion to ensure each entity is showing growth in their respective circles.

Yet, when has there been a time when school leaders (principals, vice-principals, supervisors, department heads, etc.) were ever examined on their mentoring ability and quality of leadership training? Mentoring needs to be "restructured" and given new purpose in the role it will play in developing our future school leaders. It should be welded in the curriculum of all school leadership programs, especially during the internship phase of a new leader's training.

The most important responsibility of a mentor is to open doors to authentic learning and assessment by delivering a problem-focused internship experience. This requires a radical and aggressive shift from mentees managing checklists and routine, mundane tasks to having the responsibility of leading a school team through the process of identifying issues in a curriculum, instruction, assessment, and finally isolating, testing, and disseminating data to find solutions (SREB, 2007, p. 24). Daresh (2001) states:

> The essence of effective administration involves the resolution of problems that people in organizations face. As a result, mentoring relationships for administrators must be directed toward the discovery of ways to refine problem-solving skills. (p. 24)

As for future applicants, mentoring should remain an integral and reinforced aspect of their professional growth and development. Universities and school districts must begin to cultivate a collective sense of professional camaraderie in order to serve their mentees well. Wilmore states:

> Team members must agree to the roles and responsibilities delegated to them. By accepting these roles and responsibilities, each member is empowered and committed to the process. Although there are multiple benefits to the team members, including their own growth and the opportunity to provide leadership to others, their first focus is to help the mentee become all he or she can be, and ultimately improve student performance. (Wilmore, 2004, p. 25)

The bottom line is that the states, universities, and school districts are ultimately responsible for ensuring an effective and accountable mentoring process. The lack of collaboration and nominal invested effort to create a "united mentoring program" are sabotaging our students and future school leaders.

REFERENCES

Brown, K., Anfara, V., Hartman, K., Mahar, R., & Mills, R. (2001). Professional development of middle-level principals. Paper presented at the annual meeting of the American Education Research Association, Seattle, WA (ERIC Document No. ED 457 595).

Crocker, C., & Harris, S. (2002). Facilitating growth of administrative practitioners as Mentors. *Journal of Research for Educational Leaders, 1*(2), 5–20. Available at www.uiowa.edu/~jrel/spring02/Harris_0107.htm

Daresh, J. C., & Playko, M. A. (1994, February). A planning model for local administrator mentor program development. Paper presented at the annual American Association of School Administrators Convention, San Francisco, CA.

Fullan, M. (2007). *The New meaning of educational change.* New York and London: Teachers College Press, Columbia University.

Ginsberg, R. (December 2008). Being boss is hard: The emotional side of being in charge. *Phi Delta Kappan, 90*(4), 292–297.

Gray, C., Fry, B., Bottoms, G., & O'Neill, K. (2005). *The principal internship: How can we get it right?* Southern Regional Education Board.

———. (2007). *Good principals aren't born—they're mentored: Are we investing enough to get the school leaders we need?* Southern Regional Education Board.

Lovely, S. (2004). *Staffing the principalship: Finding, coaching and mentoring school leaders.* Alexandria, VA: Association for Supervision and Curriculum Development.

Senge, P. M. (1990). *The fifth discipline: The art & practice of the learning organization.* New York: Doubleday Publishing.

The Wallace Foundation (2007). *Getting principal mentoring right: Lessons from the field.*

Wilmore, E. L. (2004). *Principal induction: A standards-based model for administrator development.* Thousand Oaks, CA: Corwin.

Chapter Four

Catholic School Mentoring for Mission and Ministry

Mary Ann Jacobs

INTRODUCTION

When Jesus sent his disciples out, he counseled them two by two; hence, the concept of mentoring in the Catholic faith and parochial schools is built on this principle of establishing and building a learning community that supports the new teacher or principal. Mentoring in a Catholic school addresses three areas of development for the new candidates that are (1) spiritual, (2) pedagogical, and (3) professional.

The Catholic schools' new teachers and principals are mentored for mission and ministry. During the first three years in a Catholic school, new teachers and principals are paired with more experienced colleagues who support them in a journey, as they come to understand and value teaching and administration as a mission and a ministry. These initial experiences strongly affect the long-term success and satisfaction of these candidates and the impact they have on the lives of those for whom and with whom they minister.

Qualified and competent senior teachers on staff within the same school can mentor the new teachers in a Catholic school. Another practicing principal within the diocese, on the other hand, helps the new principal. Both teacher and principal belong to a larger community of professionals who also assist with the mentoring program, thus enlarging the community of Catholic school educators.

UNIQUE QUALITIES OF TEACHING AND LEADING IN A CATHOLIC SCHOOL

Before one even enters the building, the mission of St. Mary's School is displayed on the building: *Our mission is to respect, inspire, and teach as Jesus did with our faith community*. That mission permeated every inch of the building from within as each student, PK–8, and every teacher and staff member, could recite the mission, but more importantly talk about the mission and demonstrate the mission in action.

This sense of mission is not unusual in Catholic schools and other faith-based schools. These schools were founded for a specific purpose and most often are associated with a larger faith community. Back in 1990 and then again in 2005 the Catholic bishops of the United States issued a statement affirming the strong conviction that Catholic schools are of great value to the Church and to the nation.

They affirmed that Catholic schools afford the fullest and best opportunity to realize the fourfold purpose of Christian education, namely to provide an atmosphere in which the Gospel message is proclaimed, community in Christ is experienced, service to our sisters and brothers is the norm, and thanksgiving and worship of our God is cultivated (U.S. Conference of Catholic Bishops, 2005a). With this purpose in mind, mentoring in the Catholic school relates to the development of those who are leaders in these schools—principals and teachers.

To understand how mentoring in these schools may be different from other non-faith-based schools, one must understand the typical Catholic school. In the third millennium, most Catholic schools are PK–8. With more than five thousand schools in the United States today, mean enrollments are 200–300 students in a PK–8 setting. Most Catholic schools have one administrator in the school and often only one of each grade level within the school. Most principals know every student by name, and often teachers do too. Every teacher knows every other teacher.

These small communities have advantages and disadvantages. Teachers and occasionally the principal are quite likely to know their colleagues beyond the school environment. Teachers and the principal may belong to the same church, recreate at the same local gathering spaces, and shop at the same stores. Teachers and the principal may have children who are friends with the children of other teachers, or may have their children in the same school where they teach and thus have colleagues who are teaching their children. While most of these acquaintances can result in a stronger sense of community, these close acquaintances can also result in colleagues knowing more than is necessary about each other. When mentoring in a Catholic school, a professional stance is critical to both mentor and mentee.

TIM, THE TEACHER, AND HIS MENTOR, JENN

When selecting a mentor for new teachers, the principal begins with the choice of the best teachers. Jennifer was the pre–K teacher for seven years at St. Mary's and prior to teaching PK she taught first grade for three years. Jenn was the ideal early childhood teacher. She knew how to strike a balance between being warm and loving with these children in their beginning years and yet firm and consistent so they would learn.

Tim was a brand new teacher. Teaching was his second career. For the previous five years he was the stay-at-home-dad while his wife continued her professional career. This was a mutual agreement as Tim wanted to pursue a teaching career, but the birth of their youngest son Tommy, who was now beginning kindergarten, necessitated one parent to stay at home. The decision was an easy one. Tim stayed home during the day with his son while his wife was at work and his older two children were in school. He pursued his teacher education degree in evening classes in an alternate-route pre-service program. With Tommy ready to start kindergarten, Tim was ready to begin his teaching career.

The stay-at-home-dad routine prepared Tim in many ways to begin his career as a kindergarten teacher. Tim had spent the previous year preparing Tommy to embrace school. In addition to working with Tommy, Tim also taught religion classes to seventh graders in his local church. This gave Tim an opportunity to meet the needs of a different age group and note the differences between five-year-olds and twelve-year-olds. Tim also was the coach for his other son's little league team.

When selecting a teacher mentor in a Catholic school, several considerations are made, based on the research findings that support effective mentoring: physical proximity, grade level and/or subject matter matches, personal compatibility, and commitment to the mission of the school (Public Education Network, 2003).

Based on these considerations, selecting Jenn as Tim's mentor seemed to be the most logical choice. Jenn had taught a grade above and a grade below kindergarten, and had a balanced approach in the classroom that produced competent and confident students. She knew the new kindergarten class, as most of the students had been in her PK class. Jenn was a great role model for the kind of teacher St. Mary's espoused.

However, one issue made Jenn less than the perfect mentor. She and Tim were good friends. Tim was her son's little league coach. Tim's daughter and Jenn's daughter took skating lessons together. Tim's family and Jenn's family had membership in the same community pool and spent considerable time together in the summer.

Recognizing this friendship as a possible challenge, we reexamined our commitment to giving support to new teachers. As much as possible, St. Mary's staff agreed to give new teachers the following supports: (a) limited teaching responsibilities so the new teacher could focus on the assigned class or subject matter; (b) support in gathering and using appropriate instructional materials; (c) limited additional workload for the mentor teacher; (d) shifting (when possible) to more experienced teachers those students who create problems beyond the abilities of the new teacher; (e) specialized instruction concerning the community of the school and the students the new teacher is likely to encounter; and (f) a collaborative professional learning community (PLC). St. Mary's staff was committed to respect, inspire, and teach as Jesus did in working with its newest staff members.

And so the staff made the words of the master teacher real: "You call me 'teacher' and 'master,' and rightly so, for indeed I am. If I, therefore, the master and teacher, have washed your feet, you ought to wash one another's feet. I have given you a model to follow, so that as I have done for you, you should also do" (John 13:13–15). The staff shared responsibility for the success of these new teachers. Jenn agreed that personal friendship in this case may be the best support for Tim.

Induction Days for New Teachers

Each year in which there were new teachers, a staff induction was held in early August. Staff induction included a two-day gathering of new teachers and mentors. The first morning of the induction was a retreat that focused on the mission of the school and the mission of the Catholic school teacher. This retreat theme of mission was revisited several times during the school year at regular faculty meetings as well as during new faculty gatherings. Each new teacher was given a copy of Stephen Covey's *Seven Habits of Highly Effective People* and the corresponding personal notebook. These books were used for personal reading and reflection as well as group sharing. By the end of the first year, new teachers completed the exercises in the notebook that prepared them to write their personal mission statement.

The second part of this induction day was spent in the new teacher's classroom. During this time the new teacher and mentor talked about classroom management. Depending on the grade level, a classroom layout plan was developed and mentor and mentee arranged the room. Discussions on classroom procedures led to the establishment of some basic routines for entering and leaving classrooms, fire drill, homework policies, and other topics, which would be essential for the safe and orderly classroom behaviors. Classroom order was addressed and preliminary plans were made for bulletin boards and displaying instructional materials. Before the close of the first day, the new teachers were given curriculum plans and the schedule for classes for their grade level.

The next morning new teachers and mentors focused on curriculum, including yearly goals, schoolwide assessments, and the development of lesson planning and delivery. The mentors worked with new teachers in developing the first week of lesson plans using the classroom texts in conjunction with the curriculum plan for the specific grade level.

In the afternoon session on the second day, mentors and teachers examined the school calendar for the year. The calendar would serve as a guide for meetings throughout the year. During this induction session, the first quarter was the focus. The mentors helped teachers work backward from the end of the first quarter when grades were due. They tentatively scheduled the curriculum based on four quarters and made plans for this quarter. They set up plan books indicating any events and/or holidays during the quarter so the new teachers would know what to expect. The day concluded with plans for the next several weeks of tasks that needed to be completed to successfully begin the new school year.

Mentoring through the Year

Jenn and Tim made plans for working at school one day a week on the same day for the next several weeks. This would allow Tim to ask Jenn questions as he continued to plan for the start of the school year and allow Jenn to monitor Tim's progress as the start of school approached.

With the induction days as a beginning, the mentoring continued the process for supporting the new teachers. There were several scheduled meetings that were a part of the mentoring program. In the first week of school, new teachers met with mentors each day for a debriefing of the day. This session was typically 20–30 minutes and allowed the new teachers to ask questions and seek assistance as needed. In the second week, new teachers and mentors met twice, and then they met weekly from the third week through the remainder of the school year. This meeting generally took place during one of their common planning periods.

St. Mary's had at least two common planning periods each week for grade-level teachers. Tim and Jenn were in the PK–Grade 2 PLC. The one common planning period for the PLCs included all the teachers in that grade cluster. This enabled the new teachers to collaborate with other teachers and learn from an extended community. All teachers met together each month for faculty meetings, which again enlarged the community of learners.

The school calendar was briefly reviewed at each of these meeting sessions and explanations of upcoming events and teacher expectations were addressed. This constant overview of what was to come allowed the new teachers to have a greater sense of what to expect.

Professional development was constantly in place for the new teachers. Each monthly faculty meeting had professional development on a specified topic. In addition to the monthly faculty meetings, three times throughout the year all new teachers in the diocese came together for spiritual, pedagogical, or professional development. This opportunity allowed teachers like Tim to connect with other new kindergarten teachers and network with them.

Throughout the year, Jenn and Tim visited each other's classrooms to observe how each taught and interacted with students. Eventually Tim branched out to visit the classrooms of other teachers, most often those in his PLC cluster.

Meeting the Needs of the New Catholic School Teacher

Not every induction and mentoring program was exactly like the program at St. Mary's, although common elements existed in each program throughout the diocese such as the spiritual, pedagogical, and professional development of the new teachers. The common diocesan days for new teachers were established for all new teachers. What happened in each school was unique to the culture of the school. In addition to the uniqueness of each school, there was also the uniqueness of each new teacher.

Tim was not in the "fresh out of college" new category. Tim had a former career. Tim had a skill set for working with colleagues and taking initiative. Tim had a sense of responsibility that can only be learned with experience. Tim did not need the emotional or psychological support that is often needed by new teachers in their first career. Tim needed support that focused on instruction to develop his pedagogical skills. His match with an experienced teacher who was familiar with developmentally appropriate strategies for addressing the need of the five–year-old supported him in his growth as a teacher.

Jenn was not in a position to evaluate Tim. They were in a collegial position—learning from each other. This relationship allowed Tim to make mistakes that would not be held against him. This also allowed him to ask questions, try something new, and admit what did not work.

Throughout the year Jenn and Tim could be observed working together. They would discipline together, observe and reflect together, plan curriculum, rehearse parent meetings, and even bring their classes together for holy day and holiday celebrations.

Mentoring Beyond the First Year

What occurred in the first year of Tim's mentoring continued in his next two years as a kindergarten teacher. The relationship that develops between mentor and mentee often results in a lifetime of professional sharing. For Tim and Jenn, they were friends before they started working together. By the end of Tim's first year as a teacher, they had become colleagues. For the next two years, Jenn and Tim continued to meet on a regular basis. Each week they would meet with their colleagues in their PLC groups.

In addition to those meetings, Jenn and Tim met at least once a month to continue their collegial sharing in the ministry of Catholic school teaching. While the mentoring program is officially designed for a three-year period, when the mentoring program is effective, this relationship of colleagues lasts much longer. The intent is to create a community in Christ, one that shares in faith development of young people. However, the community of believers strongly impacts all learners. For Jesus himself said, "Where two or three are gathered in my name, there am I in the midst of them" (Matt. 18:20).

THE PRINCIPAL IN THE CATHOLIC SCHOOL

Principals in Catholic schools can be likened to the mayor of a town. The principal is responsible for everything in the school, from the legal requirements included in providing a quality education to the fiscal management that questions every building and grounds decision for fixing the leaky faucet. The principal does it all.

One of the first responsibilities of the principal is to select a mentor. Unlike mentors for teachers, the principal seeks out a colleague who will journey with the principal in leading learning. Mentors for Catholic school principals are most often selected from among other principals who serve in the same diocese. Because the schools in the diocese are under the auspices of the bishop of the diocese, and more directly under the Catholic schools office, it is in the new principal's best interest to select a principal who has experience as a learning leader in the diocese.

MARIA, THE PRINCIPAL, AND HER MENTOR, CHARLENE

Maria asked Charlene, who had served as principal in her current school for more than ten years, to be her mentor. Maria had worked with Charlene on various academic committees prior to assuming her leadership role at St. Mary's. Their schools were in close proximity to each other and thus were in the same diocesan region. The principals in the region had monthly meetings to discuss current issues and work together on school-level and diocesan-wide projects.

The principal's mentor was very different from the mentor for a new teacher. Charlene served most often as the voice on the other end of the phone who could answer Maria's practical questions such as how to complete a diocesan form. She also served as the voice of experience in working with teachers, parents, and diocesan and district personnel. Although Charlene was Maria's designated mentor, all the principals in the region became types of mentors to the new principal.

The monthly meetings were a most supportive component for the new principal. These meetings were conducted by principals for principals. These were opportunities for colleagues to collaborate with colleagues.

In addition to the monthly meetings, five times during the year all principals of the diocese gathered for meetings. These meeting opportunities addressed recent developments within the diocesan schools such as accreditation, curriculum development, and personnel issues. One of those gatherings was always a two-day retreat for all principals, which included an overnight stay allowing all principals to socialize on another level, and in a non-school meeting place. The spiritual as well as the professional gatherings were a major form of mentoring for the new principal.

Mission-Driven Leadership

The principal stands alone when facing day-to-day tasks that require immediate decisions. Although a mentor may be only a phone call away, the principal has to be able to lead from the position the principal has.

Prior to assuming the role of principal, Maria had been a Catholic school teacher for nine years. She taught primary and middle school levels in two Catholic schools in different dioceses. Maria had been identified by her former principal as an educational leader and she recommended her for the Catholic School Leadership Program. This program within the diocese was established in response to an ongoing need to recruit and prepare future Catholic school leaders.

As the Church leadership explained:

> Among the baptized, all of whom are called to serve the mission of the Church, some experience a further specific call to lay ecclesial ministry. The call may come in a dramatic moment. More often, it comes as the person grows—within the community of faith—in love for God and a desire to do His will. One

considers that the graces received could now be put in service to the Church. (U.S. Conference of Catholic Bishops, 2005, p. 29)

This was the case with Maria. She joined the leadership program a year prior to accepting the principal position at St. Mary's. As a part of the program, Maria collaborated with other potential and new principals. The program focused on three areas of leadership: leading self, leading others, and leading with others.

> School leaders . . . must be learning leaders . . . leaders of learning in the classroom, the school, the district and who constantly are learning to lead better. It is this kind of leadership that supports and enhances the mission of the school: to provide a quality education that is based on and grounded in lasting principles and is delivered in a supportive educational environment. (Kushner, 1997, p. 81)

This program was a major part of the mentoring program for all new principals. During the first year of the program with an emphasis on leading self, Maria developed her personal mission statement. With this experience, she was able to reflect on the mission statement of her new school and assist her teachers in developing their own personal mission statements. Mission served as the basis for all decisions within the school, and it was her personal mission and the mission of the school that served as the framework for leading herself, leading others, and leading with others.

The Twelve-Month Survival Guide

One aspect of the mentoring program for new principals that became the principal's "bible" was what was known by all new principals as the principal's binder. This practical guide was divided into twelve sections—one section for each month of the year. The guide began with July—the month the principal officially began her ministry in the Catholic school and the month the principal went to "boot camp for new principals." This one-week intensive orientation for new principals included some directives for all the contents in the binder.

Behind the July tab was a list of summer activities principals needed to address to be ready to begin the new school year. Among the summer tasks would include creating schedules, interviewing and hiring new teachers, planning the school calendar for the year, and reviewing any orders—textbooks, office and school supplies, and maintenance materials—that may have been ordered or still needed to be ordered. In addition to the list of tasks were resources for completing the tasks such as interview questions for hiring new teachers and diocesan holidays and holy days for the calendar. Phone numbers and email addresses were included for all diocesan staff and for all principals in the diocese.

As a part of this week-long orientation, new principals had opportunities to engage in several of the tasks listed behind the July tab. New principals role-played interviewing teachers and checking on teacher references. Calendars were developed by each new principal with a template that was adaptable enough to be used in any school. The letters of welcome to faculty and parents were created so these would be ready for the new principal to send in early August.

During the week, time was spent on examining each month and noting the tasks principals would do during the year. In addition to the July tasks, time was spent fully examining the August and September tasks as the new principals would not meet again as a group until mid-September. By then the principal had to have everything in place to successfully begin the new school year. The checklist included for each month became a guide for new principals in planning and executing required responsibilities.

One of the most beneficial aspects of this week-long orientation was the opportunity to become acquainted with all new principals in the diocese, as well as the members of the Catholic schools office. These new principals would meet regularly throughout the school year, and this social, professional, and spiritual opportunity for development during these days allowed each new principal to become part of a PLC. When new principals met throughout the year they had already developed friendships and a collegial working relationship.

The principal's binder became the outline for success for the entire year and for years to come. With each gathering during the year the new principals would review what could be anticipated for the next few months. Principals were encouraged to add their own reminders and resources to their binders—especially as the reminders related to their own schools—so they would be able to use their binders each year until the tasks and responsibilities became automatic for the principals.

The Three-Year Leadership Program

All new principals in the diocese were required to participate in the Catholic School Leadership Program. Maria had been a part of the three-year program a year prior to becoming a principal. She had completed one segment of the program—leading self. When she became a principal she continued with the cohort of learning leaders with whom she began the program.

The three-year leadership program was arranged cyclically so that participants could enter the program in any year. Year A focused on leading self, Year B focused on leading others, and Year C focused on leading with others.

Maria was in Year B—leading others. Major components of this segment of the program included a focus on communication, designing and conducting effective meetings, team building, uncovering and discovering talent, delegating by designing and not dumping, seeking common ground, and using criticism (Kushner, 2014). For new principals these were critical skills and dispositions to be developed and practiced. As a teacher, Maria worked with some adults including her colleagues and students' parents and guardians. As a principal, she was working almost exclusively with colleagues.

This segment of the program enabled her to lead others by leading herself as she verbalized her mission and the mission of the school, set goals, created strategies, and developed skills for time management, made and kept promises, and became a disciple of principles and teachings that required an orientation toward excellence (wanting always to surpass personal best), chose those behaviors and participated in those activities that enhanced dignity rather than diminished them, and those that drew people together rather than separated them, discriminated against them, categorized, or stereotyped them (Kushner, 2014).

In the third year of the program, Maria would develop the knowledge, skills, and dispositions to lead with others. She would learn and practice ways to engage stakeholders, seek common ground, design organizational tasks, make small incremental change early enough in a large process to produce substantial results, begin with the end in mind, get the right people in the room, and synergize.

Principal among Principals —
A Member of the Larger Community

Most people want to belong to something larger than themselves. This is often the case with Catholic school principals. These principals practice what is referred to as transcendental leadership. In this relationship, leaders promote unity by providing equitable exchange rewards, appealing to the intrinsic motivation of associates with whom they work and by developing their transcendent motivation—that is, the motivation to do things for others (Cardona, 2000). The notion of service demands that one give of one's best to others. Catholic school principals, motivated by a desire to serve, fundamentally give of their best to their colleagues.

Maria, as well as all new principals, was immersed in a community of learners who were committed to service and spirituality. Catholic school principals are called to lead in the spirit of Jesus Christ. This leadership is one that is based on Gospel servant leadership. Mark's Gospel indicates that the only leadership allowed within Jesus' community is servant leadership, modeled on Jesus, "who did not come to be served, but to serve and to give his life for a ransom for many" (Mark 10:45).

In Matthew's Gospel, Jesus remarks: "The greatest among you must be your servant" (Matt. 23:11). And at the Last Supper, Luke notes how Jesus tells the disciples: "The greatest among you must behave as if he were the youngest, the leader as if he was the one who serves" (Luke 22:26). John's Gospel in the thirteenth chapter records how Jesus moved from the head of the table, knelt down, and washed His disciples' feet as a sign of servant leadership (Lavery, 2012).

Catholic school principals create a community of leaders and servants. They recognize that while they are ultimately responsible for leading their own schools, they are also responsible for transforming society. This transformation is made possible when each Catholic school principal contributes to the support of the Church as a whole in supporting each principal within their own diocese. This sense of community that we are "in this together" causes these principals to self-sacrifice with those whom they collaborate.

While Maria recognized that Charlene was her selected mentor, she also knew that every Catholic school principal in her region and in her diocese was also there to support her and mentor her in her ministry and mission. This community of learning leaders modeled for her servant leadership and mentored her in modeling this for her own school community.

BEYOND MENTORING TO BUILDING THE FUTURE FOR ETERNITY

Mentoring in Catholic schools is a mission and a ministry. Teachers and principals in Catholic schools not only are responsible for academic learning, but just as importantly are responsible for the faith development of those entrusted to them.

While dioceses most often have their own induction program in place for new teachers and principals, there are common elements in most of these programs. Orientation programs that vary from one day to full-year programs are part of most mentoring programs. Most teachers and principals are paired with another veteran teacher or principal as a resource person. Learning and leadership academies are also avenues for recruiting and supporting teachers and principals (Rieckhoff, 2014).

The element that is constant for all teachers and principals in the Catholic school is the promoting of the good news. St. Paul notes that "to each is given the manifestation of the Spirit for the common good" (1 Cor. 12:7). As new teachers and principals are mentored they in turn become mentees. The common good is developed and promoted constantly in the faith community of learners. Each member of this faith community brings treasures and talents that are shared as they build the future for eternity.

> Isn't it strange that princes and kings
> And clowns that caper in sawdust rings
> And common people like you and me
> Are builders for eternity?
>
> To each is given a bag of tools
> A shapeless mass, a book of rules
> And each must build ere life has flown
> A stumbling block or a stepping-stone.
>
> (R. Sharpe, circa 1809)

REFERENCES

Cardona, P. (2000). Transcendental leadership. *The Leadership and Organizational Development Journal, 21*(4), 201–206.

Kushner, R. (1997, August). *A model for a mission.* Paper presented at the meeting of the National Council of Professors of Educational Administration. Vail, CO.

———. (2014). *Leadership at a glance: Matrix of knowledge, skills, and dispositions.* Accessed at http://home.manhattan.edu/~SBL/leadership/ksd.php

Lavery, S. (2012). The Catholic school leader: A transcendental leader? *Journal of Catholic School Studies 84*(1), 36–42.

McDonald, D., & Schultz, M. M. (2014). The Annual Statistical Report on Schools, Enrollment and Staffing. New American Bible, revised edition (2010). Washington, DC: Confraternity of Christian Doctrine.

Public Education Network (2003). *The voice of the new teacher.* Washington, DC: Author.

Rieckhoff, B. S. (2014). The development of faith leadership in novice principals. *Journal of Catholic Education, 17* (2). Retrieved from http://digitalcommons.lmu.edu/ce/vol17/iss2/3

U.S. Conference of Catholic Bishops (2005a). *Co-Workers in the Vineyard of the Lord: A Resource for Guiding the Development of Lay Ecclesial Ministry.* Washington, DC: USCCB Publishing.

———. (2005b). *Renewing Our Commitment to Catholic Elementary and Secondary Schools in the Third Millennium.* Washington, DC: USCCB.

Chapter Five

Meaning-Making Mentoring through Communication, Relationships, and Caring in Higher Education

Floyd D. Beachum

Mentoring is one of those words that has an operational definition, but is still somewhat vague, personal, and situational. It can involve advisement, support, admonishment, encouragement, opportunity, connections, and/or a listening ear. As in other fields, it is an invaluable aspect of the academy. As an academic, however, one has to consider how to navigate the local environment, build networks with other scholars, and develop a line of inquiry/scholarship worthy of national or international prominence.

The journey towards success in the academy can be loaded with political minefields, train-wrecked by sub-par teaching, and decimated by lack of dedication to the scholarly endeavor. This chapter seeks to show how to avoid such pitfalls and chart a pathway to success with three pillars of mentoring: communication, relationships, and caring.

The word *mentor* is very interesting in that it is a term that many understand, yet may find it difficult to accurately define or explain. A mentor can be described as someone with experience who offers advice, guidance, and/or counsel. The word *mentor* comes from the name of a character in *The Odyssey*. It has evolved into a term that usually describes someone who shares information and/or wisdom with another who may be less experienced or a novice. For me, mentoring is both professional and personal.

On a professional level, it is critical for gaining information, insight, and even influence. On a personal level, mentoring occurs when one has a real and genuine interest in colleagues, their career, and their well-being. The truth of the matter is that it is hard to mentor someone you do not like, thus the thrust of this chapter is about communication, relationships, and caring. Before I discuss those topics, I will address the context of higher education and also describe some different types of mentors.

THE CONTEXT OF HIGHER EDUCATION

The role of the college/university is still integral to American society, as a place of innovative research, engaging teaching, incredible discoveries, sizable grants, far-reaching partnerships, and laudable service. Faculty plays a particularly key role in the mission of the institution. "The faculty is the backbone of any college or university, and can be neither healthy nor productive if not cared for in ways that allow for a successful balance of personal and professional lives" (Philipsen & Bostic, 2010, p. xvii).

The race for more and more prominence amongst colleges and universities places additional burdens on faculty members to increase productivity. The broader ambitious pursuits of the institution could have a tremendous impact on those most vulnerable in the tenure-track hierarchy, assistant professors. Therefore, mentoring is critical.

Personal Reflections: My First Experiences

Sometimes it can be a challenge seeking out and finding a good mentor. I remember back as a new assistant professor, I was assigned a mentor within my department. This was a nice gesture on the part of the university, but the person assigned was not really in my specific field of study, nor did we have similar research interests. Therefore, this mentoring relationship was not particularly effective even though we were cordial.

Around that same time, I happened to meet a very dynamic vice chancellor at the university who had experience and was very insightful. He was not in my area of study either, but we did have similar research interests and he wanted to help me with my research agenda as well as get some pieces published. Unfortunately, he soon accepted a higher position at another university, and I was once again without a mentor. My first two years in the academy were challenging as I was trying to determine how to best spend my time, what research to do, and what conferences to attend. I soon realized that powerful mentoring can happen informally.

Mentor Example #1 — Collegiality and Support

As I was trying to find my way as a new assistant professor, I started to get to know our department chair a bit more. This person was in my field and had held many positions in our national organization, as well as at the university (even dean of the School of Education). Over time, we began working together on recruiting students, initiating new programs, and even writing a few research grants. At first, it seemed like we were just working together as colleagues (and we certainly were), but later I realized that what this person was doing was providing me with access to area school leaders, crucial visibility with local communities, and support for my research interests.

I reflected on our relationship later and realized that this person had been a staunch supporter of mine from the day I first interviewed. The interesting notion was that this person (1) did not approach mentoring as involving any kind of hierarchy and (2) did not see me as a subordinate, pre-tenure faculty member. This person was also the same one who would be sitting next to me as I faced a divisional review committee for my tenure and promotion. Although not saying much, this mentor was in the room lending much-needed support to my cause. From this experience, I began to realize that all mentors did not approach mentoring in the same way. This person believed in collegiality, support, and the facilitation of relationships to help create an environment for my success.

Mentor Example #2—Honesty and Advocacy

As I was going through the promotion and tenure process, I started attending our national educational leadership conferences (University Council of Educational Administration). At these conferences, I did not know exactly what to expect: I hoped to meet some others in situations similar to mine and maybe even some senior scholars if I was lucky. I was not prepared for what happened next. I had the good fortune to meet a senior scholar in the field who was quite candid about my situation and career trajectory. On our first meeting, this person asked me who I was, where I worked, and quickly gave me an assessment.

I was told that I needed to start coming to our national conference annually along with the annual meeting of the American Educational Research Association (AERA) in the spring. I was also told that I needed to start meeting key people in the field, establish a coherent research agenda, and write effectively and often.

This person did not beat around the bush, and I appreciated her bluntness. Unfortunately, senior faculty members can sometimes be too vague with regard to the requirements for tenure and promotion, especially at their home universities. While I certainly understand that no one can give an exact number for publications, teaching evaluation scores, or service activities, there are ways to be more concrete about expectations.

This person followed up by giving me her email and cell phone number and told me to call whenever I had a question or needed advice. This person mentored by being completely honest, sharing information, and advocating. This person was a scholar of color who had a deep commitment to making educational leadership as well as the academy a more welcoming place for everyone. This person also invested a great deal of time and energy into mentoring pre-tenure faculty.

As I attended these conferences each year, this mentor would always check with me to see how things were going, invite me to a dinner with other faculty of color, and introduce me to other key people in our field. She also encouraged me to represent my university as a Plenary Representative. For me, it provided great insight into how our national organization operated and gave me some great visibility. I recognized that sometimes we need a little extra encouragement and also opportunities. This person not only cared about me as a person, but also was interested in my success as a faculty member and how I could position myself to make a greater impact on our field and pave the way for others.

Mentor Example #3 — Focus and Political Savvy

I met this next person also at a national conference. He had an intriguing style because he had the ability to connect with multiple audiences. I saw how people were drawn to him and how he exuded kindness, confidence, and professionalism. As I was working towards tenure and promotion, this person constantly asked about how my research was going. He frequently wanted to know what I was writing. He too was very forthcoming about what typically gets judged for tenure and promotion, and by far it was research/scholarship first. Thus, I would always be ready with a summation of what I had done and what I was working on at the time.

This person also mentored me in terms of the politics of higher education. At the time he was going into higher education administration and would serve as associate dean and eventually dean. We would talk about how to work with and around people if needed. He had a kind of political savvy that was not abrasive or self-aggrandizing; in fact, it was the opposite, warm and inviting. He had the best of intentions for the organization at heart and appropriately used his power to reward, critique, complement, and/or punish.

I remember his advice to make sure that people always associated good things with your name because your name will travel ahead of you sometimes. The lesson was that people may hear about one or one's work before they even meet in person. This was more of a traditional mentor–mentee relationship, but we eventually became good friends. This mentor believed in being focused and politically astute. To this day, this person is known as a serious scholar and effective leader.

Mentor Example #4 — Opportunities and Exposure

This next person became a mentor of mine in an unexpected way. By the time I met this person, he was already well known in our field. He was a prolific scholar, a progressive thinker, and an active participant in our national organization. Out of nowhere, he contacted me to write an encyclopedia entry for a handbook that he and his colleagues were writing. I agreed and wrote for him thinking to myself that this was a great opportunity. At the next national conference, this person approached me and asked me if I would be interested in participating on a panel to discuss social justice in educational leadership.

I excitedly agreed! I later realized that I was one of two pre-tenured faculty members on a panel of full professors. It was not a problem because the senior scholars made us feel welcomed as a part of the team. We would go on exploring the topic at other conferences, and eventually our papers were revised and turned into chapters for a co-authored book. This mentor provided me and the other assistant professor with opportunities and exposure. I later realized that even when one may have good ideas, one may not always have a platform for sharing those ideas. An opportunity is one of the most powerful things that can be given to all of us in our professions.

This person would continue to invite me to speak on panels as well as write for him on other projects. He, who was not a scholar of color, took a personal interest in my success and always allowed me the freedom to express new, different, or even controversial ideas. This mentor explicitly recognized how problems like racism, sexism, homophobia, anti-Semitism, and classism negatively affected our field. His mission was to help make a positive change by utilizing social justice and allowing diverse voices to be heard. This required a certain platform, which became the conference panels and publications. This person mentored by giving opportunities and exposure.

Mentor Example #5 — Publications and Personal Connection

This last mentoring example is also more of a traditional mentor–mentee relationship. This person took an interest in me while I was still an assistant professor. I remember that he called me into his office and asked me bluntly, "What are you writing?" I replied that I had a book review to come out soon and that I was working on some other projects. This person let me know that what I was doing was not enough; if I continued at that rate, I would not keep my job. I had two choices at this point: reject the message, thank him for his time, and leave, or see what this person had to say.

I chose the latter. From that day on, we began talking about scholarship. This mentor was a very prolific writer with numerous books and articles to his credit. While he was not in my field, he actively sought out ways to include me in his research projects. The first was an article that he started and had me finish. We then sent it out for publication. I later realized that this person gave me that article to see if I was committed enough to complete the task.

I later came to him with the idea for an edited book on urban education; and this person was very diligent in helping me craft a proposal and later securing a publisher. What emerged was a great book on urban education, and we became friends along the way. For this person, mentoring involved respect, hard work, and personal connection. If I were to work with this person, he wanted to really know who I was, what I believed, and what my goals were for the future. As time went on, we continued to produce scholarship that spanned urban education, special education, educational leadership, multicultural education, and teacher education. We continue to work together to this day.

REFLECTIONS ON MENTORS AND MENTORING

Each of the aforementioned mentors influenced me in different ways. Some colleagues helped by being a sounding board for ideas or providing advice at key times. Others made suggestions in terms of whom to ask to be external reviewers for my materials. Other mentors were more hands on, wanting us to work more closely together to develop ideas, submit conference proposals, present at conferences, or produce scholarship.

I now realize that mentors make their own unique contributions to a mentee's success and sometimes a mentee may not even know that they are being mentored. An idea that I have not mentioned yet is the responsibility to mentor the next generation of scholars. Many of my mentors made it clear that all they asked was that I would do the same thing for someone else. I was to seek out a mentee or get involved with a mentoring program and keep the cycle of mentoring alive.

KEYS TO MENTORING: COMMUNICATION, RELATIONSHIPS, AND CARING

As I have worked with various mentors, I have noticed a few themes that permeate the mentoring relationship, including: *communication, relationships,* and *caring*.

Communication

Communication is a critical aspect of mentoring. It involves the sharing of knowledge, opinions, ideas, or information. In educational leadership, we realize that schools thrive—or suffer—from the effective flow or lack of communication (Fullan, 2004). I found that mentors who made themselves available by phone, email, and text were very helpful. Access to them also displayed their commitment to my success. Beachum, McCray, and Huang (2010) wrote, "Without credible communication, the hearts and minds of the people are never won" (p. 58).

This communication also includes that critical first meeting. In my experience, all of the mentors mentioned were senior scholars who were very open and friendly when it came to working with me. Some were very honest and blunt, but they told the truth with my best interest at heart. I think we all have to sometimes put aside our egos and flatten the traditional hierarchy that places new scholars in positions where they may feel like they cannot approach senior faculty. We must communicate in ways that value other and all voices, including making new scholars feel welcomed and less anxious. I believe that this is how a great new mentoring relationship could be established.

Relationships

Relationships are critical in the area of mentoring. According to Fullan (2004), "The single factor common to every successful change initiative is that relationships improve. If relationships improve, things get better. If they remain the same or get worse, ground is lost" (p. 77). Covey (1989) explained that relationship problems tend to be one of the greatest issues for modern organizations.

While Fullan and Covey were discussing modern organizations, the personal lesson is similar. In K–12 education, relationships are fundamental to teaching, learning (Kunjufu, 2002), and leadership (Beachum, Dentith, McCray, & Boyle, 2008; Kouzes & Posner, 2007). Relationships can be built on trust, connection, mutual interest, and respect. One of my early attempts at mentoring was unsuccessful. I was paired with a mentee who seemed like a nice person, but we did not have much in common.

This person was a school administrator who was basically trying to just complete the dissertation and did not have much interest in research. In addition, the person's research area was not complementary to my own. This is not to say that these things must always be in total alignment, but they do help. In a different scenario, I met someone in passing at a conference who was a graduate student, and we ended up getting along very well. This person was interested in becoming a faculty member and had research interests that were similar to mine. We knew many of the same people in our field and we just really connected. I am still mentoring this person to this day. Relationships really do matter when mentoring.

Caring

It almost seems like a cliché to mention caring as a component of mentoring; however, it cannot be understated. Starratt (1991) wrote,

> Caring recognizes that it is in the relationship that the specifically human is grounded; isolated individuals functioning only for themselves are but half persons. One becomes whole when one is in relationship with another and with many others. (p. 195)

Mentoring is a good example of a situation where people must have these kinds of human interactions that can maximize wholeness. Furthermore, Beachum, McCray, Yawn, and Obiakor (2012) indicated that caring also entails sincere dialogue; this kind of dialogue can create a two-way street with regard to caring. For the act of mentoring to take place, sincere dialogue allows for specific questions to be asked and answered with candidness and honesty.

Sometimes mentors have to be persons whom one can talk to who may not be a part of one's organization. As outsiders they can give a different perspective and not be beholden to local organizational politics. Thus, caring plays a critical role. According to Grumet (1995), our "relationships to the world are rooted in our relationships to the people who care for us" (p. 19).

REFLECTIONS ON MY MENTORING

As noted earlier, my own experiences as a mentor have been primarily positive, but with some challenges. In my experience, I have observed at least two kinds of mentoring situations. They are mentoring through pairing (being placed or paired with a mentor) and organic mentoring. Mentoring through paring is commonly part of a more formalized program usually for new people to an organization.

In my first faculty position, there was a program like this in place. Even now, I participate in a national mentoring program in my field. This approach is certainly a good idea and can be very beneficial for both mentors and mentees. The two are usually matched according to interests or some criteria that both parties have in common.

In addition, often some loose criteria are given as to how many times mentors and mentees should be in contact. For instance, a program may suggest that mentors and mentees meet or talk at least twice a semester or three times during the academic year. The problem with these kinds of programs is that the pairing does not always result in a bond or good relationship. I was paired with a mentee at another university and first met the person at a national conference (this person was a graduate student at the time). Although we got along and were cordial, our research interests were different and we could not seem to schedule convenient times to stay in contact. As previously mentioned, communication is a key aspect of high-quality mentoring. For these reasons, this particular mentoring situation did not work. In another instance, it was very effective. I was paired with someone who did similar kinds of research and we connected immediately. Therefore, the mentoring quality can be affected by the relationship between the two people.

Organic mentoring occurs when a mentor happens to meet a mentee by chance or perhaps gets recommended to a mentee by a mutual friend (and vice versa). This mentoring process may happen less often than paring because it is not formal or part of a program. The benefit here is that because there is no pressure, it allows for people to build "natural" relationships. This way people meet, talk informally, and decide where the relationship will go.

In addition, this could take place on a campus, at a conference, or in another environment. I was attending a national conference in my field and happened to meet a graduate student who just happened to know many people whom I knew. We made an instant connection and stayed in contact after that conference. We continued to meet up at subsequent conferences, and I slowly started discussing more about his research, dissertation, and applying for jobs. The mentoring relationship developed gradually over time, making the mentoring even more meaningful.

CONCLUSION

Mentoring is a dynamic, fluid, and highly personal notion. It can take many forms, with some people providing more information, support, advice, and/or opportunities. And in other cases, scholars expect honesty, respect, and a personal connection. Furthermore, mentoring relationships are strengthened by effective communication, authentic relationships, and mutual caring. While mentoring remains an intriguing concept for study and exploration, we all continue to either mentor others or be in need of a mentor.

REFERENCES

Beachum, F. D., Dentith, A., McCray, C. R., & Boyle, T. (2008). Havens of hope or the killing fields: The paradox of leadership, pedagogy, and relationships in an urban middle school. *Urban Education, 43*(2), 189–215.

Beachum, F. D., McCray, C. M., & Huang, T. (2010). Administrators and teachers sharing leadership: Utilizing C.A.R.E. in urban schools. *Making Connections, 12*(1), 51–62.

Beachum, F. D., McCray, C. R., Yawn, C. D., & Obiakor, F. E. (2012). Multidimensional leadership in urban schools. *The National Journal of Urban Education and Practice, 5*(3), 300–314.

Covey, S. R. (1989). *The 7 habits of highly effective people: Powerful lesson in personal change.* New York: Free Press.

Fullan, M. (2004). *Leading in a culture of change: Personal action guide and workbook.* San Francisco, CA: Jossey-Bass.

Grumet, M. R. (1995). The curriculum: What are the basics and are we teaching them? In J. L. Kincheloe & S. R. Steinberg (Eds.), *Thirteen questions* (2n ed., pp. 15–21). New York: Peter Lang Publishing.

Kouzes, J. M., & Posner, B. Z. (2007). *The leadership challenge* (4th ed.). San Francisco, CA: Jossey-Bass.

Kunjufu, J. (2002). *Black students—Middle class teachers.* Chicago: African American Images.

Philipsen, M. I., & Bostic, T. B. (2010). *Helping faculty find work-life balance: The path toward family-friendly institutions.* San Francisco, CA: Jossey-Bass.

Starratt, R. J. (1991). Building an ethical school: A theory of practice in educational leadership. *Educational Administration Quarterly, 27*(2), 194–203.

Chapter Six

Peer Mentoring, Coaching, and Collaboration

New Strategies for School Reform

Karen Andronico

INTRODUCTION

Although traditionally, teachers have worked alone, mainly, in their own classrooms, a growing interest in school colleagues helping each other, working in teams to develop their skills and knowledge, is trickling into U.S. education as the era of accountability becomes a stronghold in the future of American education. But schools are rarely organized or constructed to encourage teamwork in teaching, an important quality of good professional development.

Medical doctors and lawyers often work in teams, and consult over key decisions in the operating theater or courtrooms. So should and can teachers, older and newer, be enabled to keep up in their fields by working together? Moreover, which models of peer mentoring have the power to drive systematic and continuous deep learning for *all* teachers, both new and experienced, and improve results for their students? In fact, peer mentorship may be *the* key variable in sustainable school reform for the twenty-first century.

As teacher accountability intensifies across the nation in response to the implementation of rigorous Common Core standards, challenging high-stakes exams, and new teacher evaluation methods, the call for a strategy that enables teachers continuously to improve their practice so that their students' performance levels increase becomes more urgent than ever, especially since high-stakes test scores are now linked to new teacher evaluation systems. Thus, poor ratings due to low test scores could result in more teachers losing their positions.

Moreover, "top-down" observations performed by school supervisors may be stressful and even threatening to teachers, especially those new to the profession, creating cultures of fear and compliance. To make matters worse, school leaders, including principals and assistant principals, may not devote enough time to provide ongoing feedback and support for their teachers.

On the other hand, school leaders might mitigate the negative effects of harsh mandates by building the leadership capacity of their teachers and training them to work in teams to solve problems and make decisions directly affecting their students. According to Stigler and Hiebert (1999), "Teachers must be the primary driving force behind change" because "they are best positioned to understand the problems that students face and to generate possible solutions" (as cited in Wiburg & Brown, 2007, p. 1).

However, Wiburg and Brown (2007) warn that "superficial implementation could eventually" render peer mentoring "another failed educational fad" (p. 13). Fernanadez and Yoshida (2004) claim that "superficial implementation" of reform initiatives is "not likely to have any positive impact on the learning of teachers and students" (p. 13). Likewise, Reeves (2009) argues that unless there is deep implementation of strategies that involve teacher collaboration around improving student learning, school reform imperatives will fail.

Thus, models of peer collaboration in schools must be firmly embedded in the school culture if they are to be effective in school reform. However, unless school leaders understand how to create and nurture collaborative cultures, including the structures, norms, and protocols that support and sustain the work of teacher teams, teacher collaboration could prove to be another failed initiative. Most importantly, a moral imperative to close the learning gap for disadvantaged students must drive all school reform efforts.

When teachers collaborate in teams to reflect upon and receive feedback about their practice from their peers, for the purpose of improving student performance, the results can be dramatic. If supported by strong cultures of internal accountability for student achievement, where school leaders provide the necessary time and supports to teachers, peer mentoring or teacher collaboration may spearhead the strongest single movement in the history of school reform. Wiburg and Brown (2007) claim that the "power of teachers helping teachers" must be recognized as the single most dynamic catalyst in school reform (p. 2).

Three models of teacher collaboration and peer mentoring will be explored as measures for sustainable school reform: (1) professional learning communities (PLC); (2) lesson study; and (3) Critical Friends Groups (CFGs). All three models represent a cultural shift from teacher isolation to teacher collaboration and necessitate school leadership that transforms assumptions, values, and beliefs about teaching and learning. The call for change stems from federal, state, and city mandates for improved student performance; however, reform initiatives must be situated within the context of a positive culture of accountability where improved results are driven by a collective commitment to the belief that all children *will* learn, despite outside factors like poverty, and where teachers feel comfortable experimenting and taking risks to improve teaching and learning.

STATEMENT OF THE PROBLEM

Since the implementation of Public Law PL 107-110, the No Child Left Behind Act of 2001 (NCLB), test-based accountability fueled the impetus behind educational reform (Ravitch, 2010). Under the new federal mandates punitive measures would be doled out to schools that failed to meet the strict accountability mandates, squarely placing accountability for student performance on the shoulders of school leaders.

When Barack Obama took office, many educators hoped that the punitive mandates associated with NCLB would be diminished. Although Obama maintained test-based accountability as the driver of school reform, his plan held teachers, as well as schools, accountable for low test scores. Ravitch (2013) comments, "If the students' test scores went up, the teacher was an 'effective' teacher; if the students' scores did not go up, the teacher was an 'ineffective' teacher" (p. 99).

Hence, the adoption of new teacher evaluation systems linked teacher effectiveness with high-stakes test scores, making individual teachers key variables in student performance on high-stakes tests. Furthermore, Ravitch (2013) reports that economists claimed that if students had "effective" teachers for three consecutive years, the achievement test score gap between white and black, rich and poor, and Hispanic and white, would close. Now, high stakes-teacher evaluation systems would be used to sort out effective teachers from ineffective teachers, culminating in the firing of "ineffective" teachers.

In addition to meeting high-stakes mandates, a high teacher turnover rate adds another important reason for school leaders to develop and nurture a culture of peer mentoring. New teachers often report that they don't receive enough support from their supervisors because they are too busy with administrative duties. Furthermore, according to a comparison of peer mentoring and top-down teacher evaluation as professional development strategies, teachers viewed peer mentoring as "non-threatening, forward-looking and improvement oriented" while they perceived administrative evaluation as "sometimes threatening, often one-shot, and looking backward on what has happened" (National Staff Development Council, 1991, p. 11).

Because new teachers may feel more supported and trusting in a peer mentor relationship, developing a system of teacher collaboration in schools may decrease the high percentage of new teacher attrition. The National School Reform Faculty (NSRF) writes, "Recognizing the need to change the professional culture into which novices are inducted, several ambitious teacher education initiatives have linked teacher education reform with efforts to restructure schools into centers of sustained inquiry (National School Reform Faculty, n.d.)."

Currently, approximately half of the new teachers who enter the teaching force will exit it within five years. Furthermore, Miner (2014) reports that teacher turnover costs $7.3 billion a year, and "more teachers are expected to retire between 2010 [and] 2020 since any other decade since Word War II" (p. 2).

Clearly, teacher retention remains a major crisis in urban schools. Miner (2014) warns, "If we want teachers . . . who are in it for the long haul, we need to consider how to create schools that are in themselves centers for the continual learning of everyone connected to them" (p. 1). For that to happen, school leaders must change the organizational structure of their schools by distributing and sharing leadership across the organization.

THEORETICAL BACKGROUND

Organizational Theory

Shifting from a hierarchical to a lateral organizational structure, when change threatens an organization's survival, represents a change in culture. In this new culture, leaders involve constituents in decision-making, encourage their risk-taking and experimentation, value their input and ideas, trust their professional judgments, and celebrate their successes.

Cultures of Accountability

The main task of leaders when the survival of their organization is threatened is to change its culture (Fullan, 2008; Schein, 2004). Creating and nurturing a culture of internal accountability involve knowing how to engage all stakeholders in a commonly shared mission and vision (DuFour, DuFour, & Eaker, 2008; Blankstein, 2010; Deal & Peterson, 2009). According to Evans (2008), "In accountability cultures, everyone holds each other accountable for their commitments in a positive and productive manner" (p. 35). Likewise, Connors, Smith, and Hickman (2004) define accountability as a "personal choice to rise above one's circumstances and demonstrate the ownership necessary to achieving desired results" (p. 47).

Connors et al. (2004) argue for leaders to achieve accountability by aligning all actions in the organization to producing specific and measureable results. They claim that without establishing a "clear organizational result" stakeholders tend to "pursue their own individual agendas, not the company's" (p. 41). In this way, people take responsibility to identify what "wasn't working and for what they needed to do to fix it" (p. 46).

Connors et al. (2004) claim "accountability defines the foundation of all working relationships" (p. 50). Therefore, any type of peer interaction in an organization, including schools, must be situated within a culture of internal accountability where a collective commitment to improving results drives all action. In other words, the cultural shift that needs to occur during a time of organizational change is a "shift to greater accountability" (p. 49).

Shared or Distributive Leadership

To meet and exceed external demands, the role of the principal is to disperse leadership and build capacity throughout the school. To develop collective responsibility for the success of the school, the leader must train teachers to take on many of the traditional leadership roles. In this context, the principal no longer is the single authority with all of the solutions to the problems; rather, he or she empowers the teachers who are on the frontlines to make decisions and solve problems through collaborative inquiry and reflection.

Teacher Collaboration: The "Missing Link" in School Reform

According to Leana (2011), teacher collaboration is "the missing link in school reform." Elevating "social capital," or teacher collaboration, above other factors related to student achievement such as individual teacher skill (human capital), outside consultants, and the principal as the instructional leader, she claims that "the relationships among teachers . . . for improving public schools" have been widely overlooked as the major key in quality school improvement" (p. 2).

In addition, Leana states that no significant relationships were found between a teacher's formal educational training and student achievement but claims that when "social capital" (teacher collaboration) in a school is strong "student achievement scores improve" (2011, p. 2). In her study of over one thousand fourth- and fifth-grade teachers in New York City, Leana found that "students showed higher gains in math achievement when their teachers reported frequent conversations with their peers that centered on math, and when there was a feeling of trust or closeness among teachers"—teachers mentoring other teachers. Leana's study revealed that teacher collaboration was "a significant predictor of student achievement gains above and beyond teacher experience or ability in the classroom" (2011, p. 4).

Leana vividly describes what makes the difference in student achievement: "When teachers work together with their colleagues to look at student learning data, use it to determine student learning needs, and then determine their own learning needs based on what students need, they design programs that really help improve instruction. That's social capital at its finest."

Furthermore, Leana discovered from her study that in most cases teachers seek advice from one another. The results from her research showed that "teachers were almost twice as likely to turn to their peers as to the experts designated by the school district, and four times more likely to seek advice from one another than from the principal." A New York City teacher explained, "Teaching is not an isolated activity. If it's going to be done well, it has to be done collaboratively over time." But Leana is not alone in her belief in the power of teacher collaboration; researchers' findings consistently support Leana's argument concerning the importance of teacher collaboration in school reform.

Elements of Collaborative Cultures

As Fullan (2008) states, "Collaborative cultures generate greater student learning" (p. 8). According to Deal and Peterson (2009), "Success flourished in schools with a primary focus on student learning, a commitment to high expectations, and social support for innovation, dialogue, and a search for new ideas" (p. 10). Positive school cultures emphasize the idea of the school as a learning community, not just for the students, but also for the leadership, teachers, and support staff. Hence, teachers become creative problem solvers as they utilize student data to engage in a continuous cycle of inquiry, reflecting and improving their practice according to the needs of their students.

However, teacher collaboration alone does not guarantee better outcomes. Little (2006) describes "professional community" as it "refers to close relationships among teachers as professional colleagues, usually with the implication that these relationships are oriented toward teacher learning and professional development" (p. 15). Little (2006) discovered that schools with "norms of collegiality and experimentation" adapted to change better and showed higher levels of student achievement than in schools that did not possess these attributes (p. 15). In addition, Little notes that in schools where norms of collegiality and experimentation existed, that teachers were found to be "talking frequently about their teaching and how to improve it, . . . observed each other, . . . spoke in focused ways about classroom practice, . . . developed and shared materials, . . . were open to giving and receiving advice, . . . and participated in professional development, helping one another learn new ways of teaching" (p. 16).

McLaughlin and Talbert (2001) found that teachers in collaborative cultures take "collective responsibility for all student learning" (p. 139). In these cultures, where "professional interdependence, experimentation, and reflection . . . were the norms . . . student success is explicitly everyone's responsibility" (pp. 51–52). Moreover, teachers in collaborative communities placed their students "at the center" and "adapt their practices to accommodate students," embracing the assumption that it was their responsibility that all students learned (p. 56). As teacher collaboration situated within professional community became the focus of more research, the following common elements emerged:

- Element 1: Common/shared mission, vision, values, and goals
- Element 2: Collective commitment to ensuring achievement at high levels for *all* students: creating systems for proactive prevention and intervention
- Element 3: Collective focus on student and teacher learning for the purpose of improving student performance
- Element 4: Using data to guide decision-making and continuous improvement
- Element 5: Building sustainable teacher leadership capacity or shared leadership (DuFour et al., 2008; Kruse & Louis, 2007; Little, 2006; McLaughlin & Talbert, 2001).

Caring Communities

Without a deep sense of moral obligation guiding their work, teacher teams may not believe they can overcome outside factors, including poverty and segregation, which have contributed to their students' learning gaps. According to Fullan (2001), long-lasting "intrinsic" commitment evolves from a deep moral purpose, unlike external commitment that develops as a reaction to legislative mandates. Law (2005) calls upon leaders to create a "moral purpose for their schools" by creating a "collective intentionality" to ensure that disadvantaged students learn at high levels (p. 56). Sergiovanni (1996) adds that with the establishment of a caring community, leaders need to rely less on "external controls and more on the ability of teachers as community members to respond to felt duties and obligations" (p. 73). DuFour et al. (2010) concur that the work of collaborative teams must stem from a "moral imperative" to better the lives of the students they serve (p. 11).

THREE MODELS OF TEACHER COLLABORATION

If situated in positive cultures of internal accountability and grounded in the belief that all children will learn at high levels, teacher collaboration promises to be a powerful driving force in building and sustainable school reform. Therefore, school leaders must know how to create and manage collaborative cultures where shared responsibility for student achievement is results-oriented and guided by specific norms, protocols, and structures, which support a continuous cycle of improvement. Three models of teacher collaboration and peer mentorship, which reflect cultures of internal accountability, are explored: (1) PLCs; (2) lesson study; and (3) CFGs.

Professional Learning Communities

Although a commonly used term, many schools that call themselves PLCs do not function as one. According to DuFour, DuFour, and Eaker (2008), PLCs involve "educators committed to working collaboratively in ongoing processes of collective inquiry and action research to achieve better results for the students they serve" (p. 14). Hence, in a PLC, teacher collaboration and peer mentoring must be driven by targeted improvement goals where teachers strive to improve their practice through a process of problem solving and innovation. Furthermore, common values, beliefs, clear protocols, and norms guide educators to collectively seek out and refine those practices that result in student achievement gains.

According to DuFour et al. (2004), authentic PLCs exhibit the same key features: shared mission, vision, values and goals; collaborative teams; collective inquiry; action orientation and experimentation; and continuous improvement. Furthermore, they identify the three "big ideas" of a PLC as a focus on (1) learning; (2) collaboration; and (3) results orientation.

The major cultural shift in a PLC is represented by a focus on *learning* rather than on teaching. As the "fundamental building block" of PLCs, collaborative teams work "to achieve common goals . . . for which members are held mutually accountable" (DuFour et al., 2004, p. 15). In other words, collaboration represents a means to an end rather than an end in itself and manifests itself as a "systematic process in which teachers work together, interdependently, to analyze and *impact* professional practice to improve results for their students, their team, and their school" (p. 16). In this fashion, teachers serve as mentors to one another as they collectively seek to improve teaching and learning through ongoing reflective analysis of the effect of their instruction on student achievement.

To ensure the learning of all students at high levels, PLCs frame their collaborative work around the following four questions:

1. What do we want all students to learn? (e.g., curriculum, Common Core standards, skills, concepts, dispositions)
2. How will we know that they have learned it? (e.g., system of formative and summative assessments)
3. What we will do if they don't learn it? (e.g., system of interventions)
4. What will we do if they do learn it? (e.g., enrichment)

Hence, PLCs are "action-oriented" teams of teachers who continuously strive to improve the performance of their students through thorough analysis and reflection of their pedagogy. DuFour et al. (2008) call this process "learning by doing," which can only occur in a culture where innovation and risk taking is encouraged. "Learning by doing" is grounded in the premise that better results happen only by doing things differently. Members of a PLC do not accept the status quo and collectively commit to discover ways to meet achievement and improvement goals.

The major work of a PLC is to identify essential learning outcomes for students and formatively to assess students to identify which students are learning and which students are not. To gather evidence on whether the PLCs' students have learned the intended essential outcomes, the teacher teams collaboratively create common formative assessments (CFAs) (p. 28). Teams develop and analyze CFAs rather than rely solely on summative assessments, or end-of-the-unit tests, because formative assessments provide the teachers with information on student progress *while* they are learning the essential outcomes.

Therefore, formative assessments are "for learning" because teachers can adjust their instruction while they are teaching the unit if some students are not learning. In addition, formative assessment motivates students to improve their work as they receive consistent feedback from their teachers on what they need to work on to succeed.

To ensure that assessments are used for instruction, each team must use CFAs to make adjustments to their practice for students who are not learning and to provide students with the following: systematic, targeted interventions that enable them to have additional time and support to learn the outcome during the school day without taking time away from direct instruction, and to provide students with multiple opportunities to demonstrate their mastery after the intervention has been implemented. In PLCs, the learning is the constant, while time and support become the variables.

Moreover, once the team creates the CFA, the teachers must identify the level of proficiency all students must achieve by developing commonly agreed upon rubrics and analyzing student work samples together. Most importantly, the level of proficiency remains the same for each student, ensuring that the mission of learning for all students at high levels prevails. Teachers can feel comfortable doing this since they know a menu of systematic interventions has been established and will be supported by the school leaders when students are recommended for specific interventions through the analysis of CFA results.

The PLC team process can be summarized as follows:

1. Identify essential outcomes all students must learn in each content area at each grade level during this school year and during each unit of instruction.

2. Create common pacing guides and curriculum maps that each teacher will follow.
3. Develop multiple CFAs.
4. Establish a target score all students must achieve to demonstrate proficiency in each skill on each CFA.
5. Administer the common assessments and analyze results.
6. Celebrate strengths and identify and implement improvement strategies (DuFour et al., 2010, pp. 26–33).

To support the six-step process, teachers receive training, developing team norms and protocols for each step.

The collaborative culture necessary to support a PLC ensures equity and justice for all students. The implementation of Common Core standards symbolizes the nation's commitment to leveling the playing field for all students, regardless of special needs or outside factors like poverty, but without a systematic response grounded in the assumption that all students will learn at high levels in each school building, students will be subjected to random, inconsistent responses to their needs.

Lesson Study

Like PLCs, lesson study is an organizational model for teacher collaboration that focuses on improved teaching and learning, action research, improved results, innovation, and reflective practice. According to Wiburg and Brown (2007), "Lesson study is emerging in the United States as an increasingly popular form of teacher-directed professional development designed to improve . . . learning" (p. 2).

The Japanese first recognized lesson study as a means for teachers to help other teachers, embedding the system of "teachers teaching teachers" deeply into their educational culture and providing time and support for teachers to design and evaluate lessons. Defined by Yoshida (1999), lesson study is "a collaborative process in which teachers devise a research lesson, teach and observe the lesson, and then revise and reteach the lesson in an iterative cycle of professional learning (as cited in Wiburg & Brown, 2007, p. 1).

The two major goals of lesson study are to improve both teacher quality and student learning. Moreover, lesson study has proven effective in the most "poorly served schools and communities" where often the "newest and most inexperienced teachers" work (p. xviii). Therefore, this model can be a powerful strategy in closing the achievement gap.

According to a study, the "most significant predictor of students' achievement is whether their teachers had been involved in collaborative lesson and curriculum planning (Wiburg & Brown, 2007, p. xiii). Research shows that lesson study enhances teacher practice and improves student achievement (Wiburg & Brown, 2007). Therefore, this model not only serves to enhance the practice of experienced teachers but also embraces the needs of the "newest and most inexperienced teachers" with the "least professional development" who are often placed in "poor schools" with the neediest students.

Key to this model is the underlying assumption that the "research lesson" is clearly connected to student learning. The cultural shift focused on whether the students were learning, not on how the teachers were teaching. The common elements of lesson study as described below support this key principle:

1. Instruction-centered and teacher-directed: Teachers become key decision makers and problem solvers always engaged in collective inquiry and action research.

2. Scaffolding professional development: Professional development is deeply embedded in teachers' ongoing inquiry about how their students learn best, an "organized system that helps teachers to investigate their students learning" (Wiburg & Brown, 2007, p. 14).
3. Teachers deepen their subject area knowledge as a result of writing and observing research lessons and "become interested in furthering their own backgrounds" in a content area (p. 15).
4. Teachers are provided with the necessary time to support lesson study.
5. Resources to support lesson study are provided to teachers. Once teachers have identified a need for further professional development based on their collective inquiry and action research they may request "assistance from knowledgeable others" to support them in refining their practice (Wiburg & Brown, 2007, p. 16).
6. Collaborative creation of a common, standards-based curriculum that is fully aligned with instruction and assessment with "top-down" and "bottom-up" support.

The following describes the lesson study cycle:

1. Identifying a "research theme" and setting overarching goals by pointing out an area of students' weakness through the review of curriculum documents in relation to their students' learning (Stepanek, Appel, Leong, Mangan, & Mitchell, 2007, p. 59).
2. Developing a research question by clearly identifying the problem area to be addressed: For example, if the problem area appears to be that students do not seem to be able to

visualize mathematics problems, then the research question might be: Will more work with visualization of mathematical relationships help students solve fraction problems? (Wiburg, 2007, p. 26).

3. Designing the research lesson within the context of the unit being taught as well as the overarching goal: The lesson design stems from the following considerations: (a) the content students must learn; (b) the communication and discourse students will engage in; (c) the kinds of data that will be gathered to answer the research question; and (d) the principles related to engaged learning environments.
4. Teaching and observing the lesson: Two rounds of the lessons will be done and observed by the team, with the opportunity to debrief and revise after each one.
5. Debriefing, reflecting on, and revising the lesson: Immediately following the lesson, all observers will have ample time to engage in a debriefing of the lesson and the impact it had on student learning, with debriefing guidelines to ensure that the debrief is productive and positive. In two weeks, another debriefing session will be conducted for further review of the lesson where the participants watch a videotaping of the lesson and analyze the data that was collected from the lesson.
6. Sharing what was learned: During this step, teachers will share what their research has taught them regarding which instructional strategies worked best to improve student learning in a particular target area. Therefore, each lesson study team's research becomes available for other teachers to implement in their own classrooms.

Although a powerful process, without a climate of trust and respect where teachers feel comfortable in taking risks and experimenting with new instructional strategies in a continuous cycle of action research, lesson study will go the way of other school reform initiatives that were superficially implemented without the cultural change that was needed to support it.

Furthermore, Wiburg and Brown (2007) warn that the implementation of lesson study in U.S. schools "has not been smooth" (p. 11). One obstacle to deep implementation of lesson study as well as other models of teacher peer-to-peer mentorship is teachers' lack of experience in working together in a manner that results in improvement in practice and student success. Wiburg and Brown (2007) claim that "teachers had very little experience working together in substantive ways" as they traditionally functioned in isolation (p. 9). For this reason, processes, norms, and protocols must be established for teacher collaborative work.

According to Stepanek et al. (2007), "The lesson study process is more than just a means of sharing ideas" but is a way towards "developing an atmosphere in which they can regularly . . . think about and share their deeply held beliefs about teaching, how students learn, and the nature of the disciplines they teach" (p. 46). Furthermore, through lesson study, the "teachers may develop a deep sense of the intrinsic value of collaboration" and it "becomes the way that they prefer to work rather than a means of achieving specific objectives" (p. 46). In the end, teachers will choose to participate, not out of compliance, but because "being a member of the community is part of their identity" (p. 46).

CRITICAL FRIENDS GROUPS

Popularized by the NSRF, the CFG is yet another model that provides a structure within which teachers, both novices and veterans, collaborate on the effectiveness of their practice and engage in collective inquiry to improve teaching and learning. Like PLCs and lesson study, CFGs must be situated within a culture where teachers collectively hold themselves accountable for student learning as well as their own.

As defined by the NSRF, "a Critical Friends Group is a professional learning community consisting of 8–12 members who are committed to improving their practice through collaborative learning and structured interactions or protocols" (NSRF, n.d.). Hence, CFGs strongly reflect the characteristics of a collaborative school culture and, therefore, would not be sustainable unless embedded in that culture. According to the NSRF, "CFGs are about collaboration-colleagues working together to improve their work and that of their students, continually striving for excellence through shared goals, norms, and values" (NSRF, n.d.).

To change teacher and student learning, CFGs demonstrate the attributes of collaborative school cultures, including reflective dialogue, deprivatization of practice, collective focus on student learning, collaboration, and shared norms and values (Kruse, Seashore Lewis, & Bryk, 1994). Therefore, school leaders must support CFGs with the structures and processes needed to fully succeed, like times and places to meet, norms, and protocols.

Bambino (2002) states, "I could no longer blame the weather, the full moon, or my students' hormones when a lesson failed to produce its intended results. Instead, I took the work to my CFG and asked my colleagues what they saw, what they questioned, and, most important, what they saw missing in my teaching approach" (p. 25). This statement reflects the mind-set of teachers who choose not to blame outside factors like poverty, lack of parent involvement, or special needs on their students' lack of progress. Instead, they consistently reflect upon their students' progress with the support of their peers and ask for suggestions on how to improve their teaching to achieve better results.

The structure of CFGs provides specific protocols and norms for teacher collaboration and offers opportunities for colleagues to critique their own practice as well as that of their peers. Furthermore, peer mentors in a CFG collectively examine the relationship between classroom instruction and shared learning goals. As a result of peer collaboration, immediate implementation from the CFG to the classroom and back again happens as teachers continuously adjust their instruction based on the feedback they get from peers.

As conceived by the Annenberg Institute, and later developed by the NSRF, the three primary areas for collective inquiry using the Critical Friends protocols are: (1) peer observations; (2) close examination of teacher and student work using the tuning process; or (3) consulting about an issue using the consultancy process. In addition, the collegial feedback arrived at through the discussions has been grouped in three ways: "'warm' feedback consists of (1) supportive, appreciative statements about the work presented; (2) 'cool' or more distanced feedback offers different ways to think about the work presented and/or raises questions; and (3) 'hard' feedback challenges and extends the presenter's thinking and/or raises concerns" (University of Washinton, n.d.). Therefore, as in PLCs and lesson study, trust and respect play major roles in the CFG model.

General findings from studies on CFGs revealed that skilled training coaches were essential to the process, and that spending meeting time looking at student or teacher work had the most influence on teachers' thinking and practice (Dunne, Nave, & Lewis, 2000; Norman et al., 2005; Burke et al., 2011). Studies clearly demonstrate that CFGs significantly increase teacher learning, and that participation in CFGs promotes "an inquiry-oriented, practice-based, self-disclosing form of conversation" (Norman et al., 2005, p. 285). Moreover, teachers recognized how CFGs helped them to view one another as valuable resources.

In their study, Dunne, Nave, and Lewis (2011) discovered that when CFGs replaced traditional forms of professional development, participants "agreed that they had many opportunities to learn new things in their job, that they felt supported by colleagues to try out new ideas, that they were encouraged to experiment with their teaching, and that teachers in their schools were continually learning and seeking new ideas" (p. 3). Moreover, Dunne et al. found that the success of CFGs depended largely on the support they received from building administrators, emphasizing the important role of the principal in nurturing a culture characterized by "reflective practice, collaboration, shared leadership, authentic pedagogy, democracy, equity, . . . and social justice" (p. 5).

CONCLUSION

All three models of teacher peer mentorship afford opportunities for "moral school leaders" to build "moral schools." Thus, PLCs, lesson study, and CFGs become vehicles for closing the achievement gap for disadvantaged students. As shown in studies, the potential for teacher engagement and professional development is high for each of these models, and the collaborative relationships they nurture represent a "significant departure from the traditional role of teachers working in isolation" (Caskey & Carpenter, 2012, p. 60). To support this, Acheson and Gall (1987) state that "the most available source of expertise is teachers themselves: to analyze their own teaching on the basis of objective data, to observe others' classrooms and record data teachers cannot record themselves, to help one another analyze these data and make decisions about alternative strategies" (as cited in Heller, 2004, p. 81).

This concept differs from mentors or lead teachers because in this model there is no institutional level between the participants; a first-year teacher has as much to say as the experienced teacher because both novice and veteran teachers need ongoing professional development. Heller (2004) envisions a culture that fosters professional growth, where "teachers would be seen continually in each other's rooms, consulting and working together using a common vocabulary to talk about teaching and learning" (p. 82). While acknowledging the intrinsic value of the traditional model of one-to-one peer mentoring, it does not lend itself to knowledge building on a systemic scale and its sustainability may be short-lived since most of the new teacher–experienced teacher mentor models last only one year.

Although various models exist for peer mentoring and collaboration, the three models chosen for discussion prove to have tremendous potential for continuous, sustainable, and widespread school reform. Like any other obstacle to school reform, if any of the models, which require a change in school culture, is not implemented with a "long-term view," it's most likely that these reform strategies will be abandoned before they have the chance to make a significant difference in teacher development and student learning.

This work will not be easy. Building collaborative cultures of accountability, and nurturing trusting and respectful relationships among teachers, will characterize the work of school leaders. For true school reform to take hold, teachers must feel safe to bare their souls to their peers by inviting them to share the challenges they face in their practice and in their classrooms, and then accept the feedback and suggestions from their colleagues. If guided by a moral imperative, rooted in the ideals of social justice and democracy, collective commitment to improving student learning, and supported by deep implementation, peer mentorship will be a powerful force in closing the achievement gap.

Peer Mentoring and the Future of School Leadership

According to DuFour and Marzano (2009) the principal's traditional roles of supervision and evaluation are both low-leverage strategies and do not "guarantee organizational improvement" (p. 64). Dismissing teacher evaluation as "arcane and ineffective," they argue that time spent evaluating and supervising individual teachers in the classroom does little to improve student learning (p. 64). Hence, DuFour and Marzano (2009) strongly advocate that the principal's time should be spent building teachers' capacity to "function as members of high performing collaborative teams" (p. 65).

Shifting the description of their role from instructional leaders to "learning leaders," DuFour and Marzano (2009) argue that principals should be spending their time meeting with teams and asking for artifacts of student learning, rather than focusing on formal teacher evaluations and classroom walk-throughs.

Learning leaders' conversations with teacher teams would address the following questions: How is the teaching team monitoring the learning of each student? How are members using the results of their common assessments to adjust instruction for struggling learners? How have teachers and supervisors established criteria for exemplary student work? Clearly, the conversation would focus on what students were taught and what they learned (DuFour & Marzano, 2009).

Hence, the future of educational reform depends largely on school leaders' abilities to nurture highly productive teacher teams that collectively hold themselves accountable for improved results, and are willing to take risks and experiment as they build shared knowledge of best practice together. Low-leverage practices, such as top-down supervision and evaluation, must be relinquished and be replaced with moral leadership that empowers peer mentors to evaluate and reflect upon the results of their own collective practices upon student learning.

Although current research points to teacher collaboration as the key variable in sustainable school reform, city, state, and federal governments persist in instituting teacher evaluation systems that focus solely on the ability of individual teachers to raise their students' test scores. How can teachers be expected to work in high-powered collaborative teams to improve learning for their collective students when they are being evaluated and sorted out on an individual basis? To meet and exceed external demands, school leaders must not lose sight of the power of teacher collaboration and peer mentoring in raising student achievement and must continue to learn how to create and nurture positive cultures where teachers hold themselves morally and mutually responsible for mentoring each other and improving their collective students' performance.

REFERENCES

Acheson, K. A., & Gall, M. D. (1987). *Techniques in the clinical supervision of teachers: Preservice and inservice applications (2nd ed.).* New York: Longman.

Bambino, D. (2002). Critical friends. *Educational Leadership, 59*(6), 25–27.

Blankstein, A. M. (2010). *Failure is not an option.* Thousand Oaks, CA: Corwin Press.

Burke, W., Marx, G., & Berry, J. (2011). Maintaining, reframing, and disrupting traditional expectations and outcomes for professional development with critical friends groups. *The Teacher Educator 46,* 32–52. Doi: 10.1080/08878730.2010.530342

Caskey, M., & Carpenter, J. (2012). Organizational models for teacher learning. *Middle School Journal, 43*(5), 52–62.

Connors, R., & Smith T. (2011). *Change the culture change the game.* New York: Penguin.

Connors, R., Smith, T., & Hickman, C. (2004). *The Oz principle: Getting results through individual and organizational accountability.* New York: Portfolio.

Deal, T., & Peterson, K. D. (2009). *Shaping school culture: Pitfalls, paradoxes, & promises* (2nd ed.). San Francisco: Jossey-Bass.

DuFour, R., DuFour, R., & Eaker, R. (2008). *Revisiting professional learning communities at work: New insights for improving schools.* Bloomington, IN: Solution Tree Press.

DuFour, R., DuFour, R., Eaker, R. & Karhenek (2004). *Whatever it takes: How professional learning communities respond when kids don't learn.* Bloomington, IN: Solution Tree Press.

———. (2010). *Raising the bar and closing the gap.* Bloomington, IN: Solution Tree Press.

DuFour, R., & Marzano, R. (2009). High leverage strategies for principal leadership. *Educational Leadership, 66*(5), 62–66.

Dunne, F., Nave, B., & Lewis, A. (2000). Critical friends groups: Teachers helping teachers to improve student learning. *Phi Delta Kappa International Research Bulletin* (CEDR) (28). Retrieved from http://www.pdkintl.org/research/rbulletins/resbul28.htm

Evans, H. (2008). *Winning with accountability.* Dallas, TX: Cornerstone Leadership Institute.

Eugene School District. (2014). Peer mentoring. Retrieved from http://www.4j.lane.edu/hr/teachereffectiveness/manual/peermentoring0/

Fernandez, C., & Yoshida, M. (2004). *Lesson study: A case of a Japanese approach to improving instruction through school-based teacher development.* Mahwah, NJ: Lawrence Erlbaum.

Fullan, M. (2001). *Leading in a culture of change.* San Francisco, CA: Jossey-Bass.

Fullan, M. F. (2008). *What's worth fighting for in the principalship.* New York: Teachers College Press.

Heller, D. (2004). *Teachers wanted: Attracting and retaining good teachers.* Alexandria, VA: Association for Supervision and Curriculum Development.

Kruse, S. D., & Louis, K. S. (2007). *Building strong school cultures*. Thousand Oaks, CA: Corwin Press.

Law, B. (2005). Creating moral schools: The enabling potential of critical friends groups. *Educational Horizons, 84*, 53–57.

Leana, C. R. (2011, Fall). The missing link in school reform. *Stanford Social Innovation Review*, 30–35.

Little, J. W. (2006). *Professional community and professional development in the learning centered school*. Washington, DC: National Education Association. Retrieved from http://www.nea.org/assets/docs/HE/mf_pdreport.pdf

McLaughlin, M. W., & Talbert, J. E. (2001). *Professional communities and the work of high school teaching*. Chicago: University of Chicago Press.

Miner, B. (2008). Teaching's revolving door. *Rethinking Schools, 23*(2), 6–10.

National School Reform Faculty. (n.d.). What is a CFG? Retrieved from http://www.nsrfharmony.org/

National Staff Development Council (1991). Peer coaching. Retrieved from www.ncsall.net/fileadmin/resources/teach/mentor_b.pdf

Norman, P., Golian, K., & Hooker, H. (2005). Professional Development Schools and Critical Friends Groups: Supporting Student, Novice and Teacher Learning, *The New Educator, 1*(4), 273-286, DOI: 10.1080/15476880500276793

Public Law PL 107-110, the No Child Left Behind Act of 2001. Retrieved from http://ww2.ed.gov/policy/elsec/leg/esea02/index.html

Ravitch, D. (2010). *The death and life of the great American school system: How testing and choice are undermining education*. New York: Basic Books.

———. (2013). *Reign of error*. New York: Alfred A. Knopf.

Reeves, D. B. (2009). *Leading change in your school*. Alexandria, VA: Association for Supervision and Curriculum Development.

Schein, E. (2004). *Organizational culture and leadership*. San Francisco, CA: Jossey-Bass.

Stepanek, J., Appel, G., Leong, M., Mangan, M. T., & Mitchell, M. (2007). *Leading lesson study*. Thousand Oaks, CA: Corwin Press.

Stigler, J., & Hiebert, J. (1999). *The teaching gap*. New York: Free Press.

University of Washington (n.d.). Critical friends: A process built on reflection. Retrieved from https://depts.washington.edu/ccph/pdf_files/criticalfriends.pdf

Wiburg, K., & Brown, S. (2007). *Lesson study*. Thousand Oaks, CA: Corwin Press.

Yoshida, M. (1999). Lesson study: A case study of a Japanese approach to improving instruction through school-based teacher development (Unpublished doctoral dissertation). University of Chicago.

Chapter Seven

Leadership Practices in Mentoring

Richard Savior

INTRODUCTION

Mentoring has been around since time immemorial as leaders have guided the learning and development of their followers. Mentoring involves a dynamic relationship between two individuals and can be beneficial to both the mentor and the mentee. The values inherent in such exchanges are derived from relationships that are usually hierarchical in nature and are centered on the concept of learning and growth (Bowman, Kite, Branscombe, & Williams, 1999; Margolis & Romero, 2001).

Many definitions speak to coaching and counseling as critical elements, which foster and define the learning, typically from the mentor to the mentee. A common denominator to many well-established mentoring programs is a focus on establishing relationships or partnerships that aim to assist mentees in their development and in overcoming challenges, working through a structured process of improvement (Dawson, 2014). In a study of mentoring in higher education, Nakamura, Shernoff, Hooker, and Csikszentmihalyi (2009) observed:

> It can be argued that when mentoring encourages novices to strive for excellence and care for the ethical commitments and basic purpose of their profession, the experience contributes in an essential way to their subsequent pursuit of work that engages them personally, strengthens the profession, and furthers the welfare of the communities they serve. (p. xviii)

In its fullest expression, mentoring goes well beyond simple advising as most academics would define it (Creighton, Creighton, & Parks, 2010). While academic advising involves setting goals, fitting programs to interests and abilities, and evaluating progress, mentoring is far more relational with an emphasis on socialization and support (Gaffney, 1995). An understanding of mentoring in the academy is influenced by a number of factors, including institutional tradition, context, and delivery. With that having been said, certain universal components of effective mentoring support the concepts, asserting that mentoring is a managed process; that it involves human behavior and relationships; and that it incorporates elements of planning, organizing, directing and leading. This final element—leadership—is the focus of this chapter.

MENTORING IN ACADEMIA

Academic mentoring, through the expression of scholarly inquiry and intellectual tasks, encompasses many aspects of leadership inclusive of designing courses, facilitating learning activities, assessing learning outcomes, and exploring new pedagogical ideas (Hutchings, Huber, & Ciccone, 2011). Effective mentorship is not simply a matter of good technique but is also a function of the identity and integrity of the mentor as teacher (Palmer, 2007). Mentors lead their students in part by interweaving their thoughts and actions by continually questioning how they are supporting their students.

The most effective mentoring relationships emphasize active, self-directed learning on the part of the mentee, and working in a collaborative partnership with the mentor to pursue the mentee's own goals. Mentors help facilitate this transformational learning throughout this process, both through direct leadership and by encouraging and nurturing self-directed actualization in their students (Zachary, 2009).

Establishing collaborative relationships between the mentor and student is a critical element in effective mentor leadership. The collaborative aspect of such relationships implies a challenge to the traditional hierarchal arrangements of expert and novice, going beyond the mentors simply dispensing knowledge, to achieving a sense of balance in providing the student with support while encouraging the student's independence. It is tempting for mentors to rely purely on their own expertise and to be too prescriptive with students. In developing truly collaborative relationships with students, mentors need to engage in active listening while encouraging their students to develop and articulate their own positions.

While pursuing the goal of establishing collaborative relationships with students, mentors need to be aware of and manage the challenges of setting boundaries. These include deciding how much to do on behalf of students, providing support when students' academic and personal difficulties conflate and blur, and establishing an appropriate communication style that is both professional and warm and caring. Mentors need to acknowledge that they alone may not be the exclusive resource and solution to all of their students' challenges.

PRINCIPLES OF EFFECTIVE MENTORING

Certain principles guide effective mentorship. Mentors are well served to acknowledge that what they believe they know about their students is only provisionally true. It is difficult to know a priori what our students need, what they are curious about, or how they learn best. Students often surprise and inform mentors about themselves as learners and the knowledge and interests they possess. All students learn when their curiosity is engaged, so mentors need to be attentive listeners. Anderson and Shannon (1988) found that mentoring involves a high degree of personal focus . . .

> in which a more skilled or more experienced person, serving as a role model, teaches, sponsors, encourages, counsels and befriends a less skilled or less experienced person for the purpose of promoting the latter's professional development. Mentoring functions are carried out within the context of an ongoing, caring relationship between the mentor and protégé. (p. 40)

Effective mentors possess a strong sense of self-management and interpersonal relationship skills. According to Goleman (1998), a major factor influencing those qualities—and by extension, the leadership capabilities of the mentor—is the emotional intelligence of the leader. Goleman defined emotional intelligence as a function of self-awareness, self-regulation, motivation, empathy, and social skill. In terms of the self-management focus, mentors need to establish and project the sort of skills and other qualities that they are trying to impart to the mentees.

THE ROLE OF LEADERSHIP IN MENTORING

Leadership involves guiding and supporting others' growth and development; thus it can be argued that mentoring and leadership are inextricably linked. There are many ways to define leadership in the context of academic mentoring. According to McCaffery (2010), leadership is associated with the path or course one guides another on a journey, thus inferring progressive movement. Taylor, Peplau, and Sears (2006) observed that leadership usually refers to the social influence of individuals who guide or inspire others in the right direction. Davis (2011) stated that leadership implies movement, solving problems, and building capability.

Bass and Stogdill's (1990) analysis of over three thousand studies on leadership provides a number of broad conceptualizations to the practice. Common to most definitions are the concepts of process, influence, group context, and goals (Bensimon, Neumann, & Birnbaum, 1989). Northouse (2009) noted that leadership involves a process, coupled with a degree of influence, and is directed toward accomplishing some task or goal.

The expression of leadership frequently involves influencing others and creating a vision for change (Bennis & Nanus, 1985). What constitutes good leadership may be debatable, but leadership in the context of mentoring is generally considered effective when it enables students to adapt to change and move to a place where they and others are constructively better off (Kotter, 1990).

Effective mentors understand the importance of context and know that their effectiveness can be affected by the environmental and cultural conditions, the relative strength of collaboration reflected in their institution's culture, and the leadership challenges being addressed (Astin & Astin, 2000). These leaders have the ability to modify their actions accordingly, in response to unique institutional characteristics (Birnbaum, 1992).

Kezar, Carducci, and Contreras-McGavin (2006) stated that leadership has evolved over the past few decades from being hierarchical and emphasizing power to an approach that is more connective, collective, and context/process centered. Many leadership theorists share the understanding that effective mentorship is founded on a relationship and represents an interactive process that entails social processes, practices, and engagements through which followers respond to the influence of leaders and leaders respond to the needs and values of their followers (Morrill, 2007).

TRANSFORMATIONAL LEADERSHIP APPLICATIONS IN MENTORING

Mentoring is about informing, advising, guiding and otherwise helping the mentee identify and set a course for transformative personal and academic change and growth. Given that context, of the many possible leadership theories that may be applied to mentoring, transformational leadership is an arguable model to consider.

The very nature of transformational leadership theory is consistent with the behaviors that are essential to effective mentoring: individualized consideration to a follower's needs for achievement, growth, and development; idealized influence or personalized charisma that supports the mentor as role model; inspirational motivation to inspire followers; and intellectual stimulation to help followers recognize and develop their innovative abilities (Scandura & Schriesheim, 1994).

A distinguishing characteristic of transformational leadership lies in its allocation. "In transformational leadership, authority and influence are not necessarily allocated to those occupying formal administrative positions. Rather, power is attributed by members to whoever is able to inspire their commitment to collective aspiration" (Leithwood & Duke, 1999, p. 49). Academic leaders themselves are transformational when they increase the collective awareness of what is right, good, and important, when they help elevate followers' needs for achievement and self-actualization, when they foster higher moral maturity, and when they help their students consider what is good for the greater society (Tourish, 2008).

Implicit to the application of transformational leadership is the premise of change, the creation of a new perspective and the institutionalizing of that system, and some form of transition that entails the unmaking of past policy and practice, followed by a remaking of new structure, purpose, goals, or behavior while establishing a new sense of social contract and community (Eisenbach, Watson, & Pillai, 1999). According to Goldring, Crowson, Laird, and Berk (2003), the early transitional stage of transformational leadership involves the process of passing from one state to another, acknowledging that loss is integral to change. Goldring et al. (2003) underscore the need for bridging from the old state to the new, while emphasizing the need to ensure balance of continuity and change in guiding students through their development and transformation.

BENEFITS OF EFFECTIVE LEADERSHIP IN MENTORING

Howarth and Rafferty (2009) found that transformational leadership establishes a relationship between the trust that employees have in their leaders and the extent to which they embrace change. This perception of an underlying basis and process of trust and fairness is a critical element according to Atuahene-Gima (2005), as followers need to overcome both passive and active resistance to change. As a consequence, transformational leaders are more likely to be effective when they treat their followers in a consistent manner that reflects the values of others. As this relates to the faculty-as-mentor–student relationship, students realize confidence and success when they believe that mentors care about them and support their interests and aspirations.

Fisher (1996) noted that, while transformational leaders believe in collaboration, it is only with the proviso that individual (student) accountability is equally important and critical. Supporters of the transformational leadership style (Hogan, Curphy, & Hogan, 1994; Sagie, 1996; Sagie, Zaidman, Amichai-Hamburger, Te'eni, & Schwartz, 2002) point out that a highly directive style encourages followers to accept challenging goals established by their leaders and are able, in turn, to achieve their objectives.

Today, academic mentors face a broad array of significant challenges, encompassing many values and objectives, including instilling a supportive environment where students can learn and prosper, to encourage collaboration between various people(s), and to create a sense of community that reflects a sense of mutual respect and shared values. In doing so, these leaders affect positive change that enhances student learning and development. In this context, academic leadership, which successfully motivates and directs others in collaborative transformations, can have a significant impact (Koen & Bitzer, 2010).

Butcher, Bezzina, and Moran (2011) stated that academic leaders need to transcend the "quid pro quo" transactional leadership described by Burns (1978), wherein leaders and followers enter into relationships for their individual reasons to demonstrate effective transformational leadership. In a study concerning the application of transformational leadership theory in education, Brown (2010) found that as a result of certain negative treatment that students receive, sometimes as a consequence of underlying social inequalities, academic leaders have the opportunity to effect. They do so by validating and incorporating students' personal knowledge and experience.

For mentor-leaders to be effective, mentoring needs to be perceived as a positive experience to both the mentor and the mentee. According to Goldstein (1993), mentees benefit in several ways from effectively led mentoring. These include receiving encouragement and building self-confidence, acquiring new or improved knowledge and skills, developing life and professional goals, being provided resources and increased visibility, and gaining knowledge and confidence on how to overcome challenging situations.

Goldstein also addressed various benefits and advantages that mentors might receive from the mentoring relationship: effective mentoring experiences can serve to further one's professional development as a consequence of learning by teaching; through the reciprocal development of skills and the attainment of goals in a caring and productive relationship; and by the returned investment of mentees who involve their mentors in their ongoing developmental activities.

Mentoring can present significant benefits for both mentors and mentees. In a study of formal mentoring programs, Chun, Sosik, and Yun (2012) determined that mentoring support and modeling had more of a positive effect on mentors than on their followers. They found that when mentors provided significant levels of support and modeling to their protégés, the mentors experienced enhanced transformational leadership behaviors and higher levels of organizational commitment, while the protégés experience increased levels of affective well-being and satisfaction. Orpen (1997) found a number of potential benefits that stem from effective mentoring activity. Mentees typically gain added confidence, learn faster and more effectively, and realize enhanced levels of satisfaction, while mentors realize a greater sense of job satisfaction, career rejuvenation, and commitment to their organization's mission.

IMPACT OF EFFECTIVE LEADERSHIP IN MENTORING

Certain leadership qualities can have a positive contribution to effective mentoring. Dukess's (2001) study found that academic leaders are more effective when they possess a sound record of success, have well-developed interpersonal skills, are reflective and compassionate, and are effective listeners who consistently communicate on the basis of trust-based relationships. Strouse, Sieverdes, and Hecht (2005) studied the effectiveness of leadership-mentor–protégé relationships as reported by college students and found that highly effective leader-mentors were perceived as adding value to students' self-discovery and reflection, personal leadership development, and the students' academic achievement and overall life success. Schuman (2007) stated that the presence of effective leadership mentoring programs can have a positive impact of follower satisfaction.

Leaders may need to serve as mentors in fully realizing their transformational leadership potential. In a study by Scandura and Williams (2004), respondents found that mentoring enhanced their transformational leadership effectiveness, job satisfaction, organizational commitment, and career expectations. In another study, Godshalk and Sosik (2000) examined whether mentor–mentee agreement regarding mentor transformational leadership behavior has a positive influence on the quality of the mentoring relationship. Their results indicated that mentoring relationships, which featured traditional transformational leadership behaviors, had a greater degree of mentoring effectiveness. Mentoring can thus have a positive impact on leadership development and effectiveness.

Middlebrooks and Haberkorn (2009) examined the potential role that mentoring can have in fostering individual leader development. They found that effective mentors conceptualize their role and activities in alignment with established leadership concepts, specifically those behaviors associated with transformational leadership theory. The study indicated a statistically significant relationship between the implicit influences and benefits associated with mentoring and the individuals' growth in psychological capital and leadership development.

Pounder's (2008) study on the effect of college faculty on their students found a positive relationship between students' perceptions of transformational leadership and the students' relationships with their professors. The individual attention and intellectual stimulation that faculty mentors provide to students, critical elements to effective transformational leadership, can be important predictors of student participation in their academic experience (Bolkan & Goodboy, 2009). Bolkan and Goodboy's research indicated a relationship between transformational leadership and student achievement, suggesting that students benefit when they perceive a personalized element to their academic study. This finding is consistent with the foundation that transformational leadership is undergirded by recognition of individual values, needs, and intrinsic motivations.

In addition to contributing to student learning outcomes, transformational leadership can have a positive influence on guiding students' ethical conduct. Academic leaders directly and indirectly help students make informed, responsible and moral decisions. A number of researchers have examined the relationship between transformational leadership and the expression of ethical behavior. Pounder (2008) stated that transformational leadership may have a greater influence in establishing ethical behaviors and traits than transactional leadership models. Carlson and Perrewe (1995) identified a similar relationship between transformational leadership and students' ethical behavior, stating that "transformational leadership is viewed as the best approach for instilling ethical behavior" (p. 5).

CONCLUSION

Developing the collaborative relationships that are at the heart of mentoring can be complex, demanding, and highly rewarding. Mentor-leaders have the opportunity to affect transformative personal and academic change and growth as they help students realize their potential. Effective mentor-leaders leverage a strong sense of self-management, well-developed interpersonal skills, and years of experience and knowledge in making a difference in their students' lives.

The qualities of effective leadership in mentoring are not always obvious and often take the form of subtle expressions and applications. As faculty, we share our knowledge, develop curricula and programs based on our authority, and engage in research that validates our credentials. In articulating and effecting difference-making leadership in mentoring, academics would be wise to acknowledge the taken-for-granted assumptions concerning the professor-as-expert, assuming instead a subtler leadership framework of collaboration, mutual respect, and discovery. Surrendering the traditional professorial role requires confidence when seen as challenging our conventional sense of academic identity (Mandell, 2011).

Effective leadership in mentoring can be challenging when perceived as competing with traditional conceptions of the professorial. As mentor-leaders, we need to give academic significance to the myriad and often seemingly small ways we are engaged with our students' aspirations, successes, and failures and embrace these opportunities for mentoring leadership as critically important aspects of our scholarly lives. By acknowledging these guiding principles of mentoring, we realize the benefit of embedding our professorial expertise with humility, and that can be a very good thing.

REFERENCES

Anderson, E., & Shannon, A. (1988). Toward a conceptualization of mentoring. *Journal of Teacher Education, 39*(1), 38–42.

Astin, A. W., & Astin, H. S. (2000). *Leadership reconsidered: Engaging higher education in social change.* Battle Creek, MI: WK Kellogg Foundation.

Atuahene-Gima, K. (2005). Resolving the capability: Rigidity paradox in new product innovation. *Journal of Marketing, 69,* 61–83.

Bass, B. M., & Stogdill, R. M. (1990). *Bass and Stogdill's handbook of leadership* (3rd ed.). New York: Free Press.

Bennis, W., & Nanus, B. (1985). *Leaders: The strategies for taking charge.* New York: Harper Collins.

Bensimon, E. M., Neumann, A., & Birnbaum, R. (1989). *Making sense of administrative leadership: The "L" word in higher education.* Washington, DC: George Washington University.

Birnbaum, R. (1992). *How academic leadership works: Understanding success and failure in the college presidency.* San Francisco: Jossey-Bass.

Bolkan, S., & Goodboy, A. (2009). Transformational leadership in the classroom: Fostering student learning, student participation, and teacher credibility. *Journal of Instructional Psychology, 36*(4), 296–306.

Bowman, S. R., Kite, M. E., Branscombe, N. R., & Williams, S. (1999). Developmental relationships of black Americans in the academy. In A. J. Murrell, F. J. Crosby, & R. J. Ely (Eds.), *Mentoring dilemmas: Developmental relation-*

ships within multicultural organizations (pp. 21–46). Mahwah, NJ: Lawrence Erlbaum Associates.

Brown, K. (2010). Preparing school leaders to serve as agents for social transformation. *School Practices, 4*(4), 349–352.

Burns, J. M. (1978). *Leadership*. New York: Harper and Row.

Butcher, J., Bezzina, M., & Moran, W. (2011). Transformational partnerships: A new agenda for higher education. *Innovations in Higher Education, 36*, 29–40.

Carlson, D., & Perrewe, P. (1995). Institutionalization of organizational ethics through transformational leadership. *Journal of Business Ethics, 14*(10), 829–838.

Chun, J. U., Sosik, J. J., & Yun, N. Y. (2012). A longitudinal study of mentor and protégé outcomes in formal mentoring relationships. *Journal of Organizational Behavior, 33*, 1071–1094. Doi:10.1002/job.1781

Creighton, L., Creighton, T., & Parks, D. (2010). Mentoring to degree completion: Expanding the horizons of doctoral protégés. *Mentoring and Tutoring, 18*(1), 39–52.

Davis, J. (2011). *Learning to lead: A handbook for postsecondary administrators*. Lanham, MD: Rowman & Littlefield Education.

Dawson, P. (2014). Beyond a definition: Toward a framework for designing and specifying mentoring models. *Educational Researcher, 43*, 137–145.

Dukess, L. F. (2001). *Meeting the leadership challenge. Designing effective principal mentor programs: The experiences of six New York City community school districts*. Retrieved from http://newvisions.org.resources/lead-chall0.shtml

Eisenbach, R., Watson, K., & Pillai, R. (1999). Transformational leadership in the context of organizational change. *Journal of Organizational Management, 12*(2), 80–89. doi:10.1108/09534819910263631

Fisher, J. L. (1996). *Presidential leadership: Making a difference*. Phoenix: Oryx Press.

Gaffney, N. (1995). *A conversation about mentoring: Trends and models*. Washington, DC: Council of Graduate Schools.

Godshalk, V. M., & Sosik, J. J. (2000). Does mentor-protégé agreement on mentor leadership behavior influence the quality of a mentoring relationship? *Group and Organizational Management, 25*, 291–317.

Goldring, E., Crowson, R., Laird, D., & Berk, R. (2003). Transition leadership in a shifting policy environment. *Educational Evaluation and Policy Analysis, 25*(4), 473–488. doi:10.3102/01623737025004473

Goldstein, H. (1993). Perspectives on research mentorship. In N. Minghetti, J. Cooper, H. Goldstein, S. Warren, & L. Olswang (Eds.), *Research mentorship and training in communication sciences and disorders* (pp. 51–66). Rockville, MD: American Speech-Language Hearing Foundation.

Goleman, D. (1998). What makes a leader? *Harvard Business Review, November/December,* 93–104.

Hogan, R., Curphy, G. J., & Hogan, J. (1994). What do we know about leadership? *American Psychologist, 49*(6), 493–504. doi:10.1037/0003–066x.49.6.493

Howarth, M., & Rafferty, A. (2009). Transformational leadership and organizational change: The impact of vision, content and delivery. *Proceedings of Academy of Management Annual Meeting,* Chicago.

Hutchings, P., Huber, M. T., & Ciccone, A. (2011). *The scholarship of teaching and learning reconsidered: Institutional integration and impact.* San Francisco: Jossey-Bass.

Kezar, A., Carducci, R., & Contreras-McGavin, M. (2006). *Rethinking the "L" word in higher education: The revolution on research in leadership.* San Francisco: Jossey-Bass.

Koen, M., & Bitzer, E. (2010). Academic leadership in higher education: A participative perspective from one institution. *Academic Leadership, 8*(1), 1–12.

Kotter, J. P. (1990). *A force for change: How leadership differs from management.* New York: Free Press.

Leithwood, K., & Duke, D. L. (1999). A century's quest to understand school leadership. In J. Murphy & K. S. Lewis (Eds.), *Handbook of research on educational administration* (pp. 45–72). San Francisco: Jossey-Bass.

Mandell, A. (2011). The expertise of humility. *All About Mentoring, 39,* 1–3.

Margoils, E., & Romero, M. (2001). In the image and likeness: How mentoring functions in the hidden curriculum. In E. Margolis (Ed.), *The hidden curriculum in higher education* (pp. 79–96). New York: Routledge.

McCaffery, P. (2010). *The higher education manager's handbook. Effective leadership and management in universities and colleges.* New York: Routledge.

Middlebrooks, A. E., & Haberkorn, J. T. (2009). Implicit leader development: The mentor as prefatory leadership context. *Journal of Leadership Studies, 2*(4), 7–22. doi:10.1002/jls.20077

Morrill, R. L. (2007). *Strategic leadership: Integrating strategy and leadership in colleges and universities.* Westport, CT: Praeger.

Nakamura, J., Shernoff, D., Hooker, C., & Csikszentmihalyi, M. (2009). *Good mentoring: Excellent practice in higher education.* San Francisco: Jossey-Bass.

Northouse, P. G. (2009). *Leadership: Theory and practice* (5th ed.). Thousand Oaks, CA: Sage.

Orpen, C. (1997). The effects of formal mentoring on employee work motivation, organizational commitment and job performance. *The Learning Organization, 4*(2), 53–60.

Palmer, P. J. (2007). *The courage to teach: Exploring the inner landscape of a teacher's life* (10th anniversary ed.). San Francisco: Jossey-Bass.

Pounder, J. (2008). Transformational leadership: Practicing what we teach in the management classroom. *Journal of Education for Business, 84*(1), 2–6.

Sagie, A. (1996). The effect of leaders' communication style and participative goal setting on performance and attitudes. *Human Performance, 9*(1), 51–64.

Sagie, A., Zaidman, N., Amichai-Hamburger, Y., Te'eni, D., & Schwartz, D. G. (2002). An empirical assessment of the loose-tight leadership model: Quantitative and qualitative analyses. *Journal of Organizational Behavior, 23*(3), 303–320. doi:10.1002/job.153

Scandura, T. A., & Williams, E. A. (2004). Mentoring and transformational leadership: The role of supervisory career mentoring. *Journal of Vocational Behavior, 65,* 448–468.

Scandura, T. A., & Schriesheim, C. A. (1994). Leader-member exchange and supervisor career mentoring as complementary constructs in leadership research. *The Academy of Management Journal, 37*(6), 1588–1602.

Schuman, L. A. (2007). *K-12 leadership mentor programs: A qualitative study of the perceptions of the participants in three suburban Pennsylvania school districts.* Philadelphia: Temple University Press.

Strouse, S. K., Sieverdes, C. M., & Hecht, U.S. (2005). Leadership mentor selection, developmental stages, and personal leadership development. *Proceedings of the AIAEE Annual Meeting,* San Antonio.

Taylor, S. E., Peplau, L. A., & Sears, D. O. (2006). *Social psychology* (12th ed.). Upper Saddle River, NJ: Merrill Prentice Hall.

Tourish, D. (2008). Challenging the transformational agenda. *Management Communication Quarterly, 21*(5), 522–528.

Zachary, L. J. (2009). *The mentee's guide.* San Francisco: Jossey-Bass.

Chapter Eight

Instant Mentoring

The Promises and Perils of E-mentoring

Rhonda S. Bondie

"Millennials," those born after 1980, bring a culture of "instant" electronic communication as they join the teaching profession. Fittingly, e-mentoring capitalizes on the digital know-how of beginning teachers offering support with a stroke of a fingertip, 24/7, through free, easily accessible new technologies. This chapter explores the promises, perils, and practices of e-mentoring aimed at the rapid development of instructional expertise, resulting in teachers with high retention rates who produce reliable increases in student achievement.

The term *e-mentoring* is defined as "the use of computer-mediated communications such as email, discussion boards, chat rooms, blogs, web conferencing, and growing Internet-based solutions" that enable mentors and beginning teachers to interact (Smith & Israel, 2010, p. 30). Consistent with face-to-face traditional mentoring programs, the primary goals of e-mentoring focus on improving student learning and developing teacher effectiveness through interactions with expert mentors (Ingersoll & Strong, 2011). However, these interactions are dramatically changed by new technologies that remove the constraints of a common time and location for communication. New technologies offer endless possibilities for e-mentoring, creating both opportunities and challenges for program design.

PROMISES OF NEW TECHNOLOGIES

One goal of e-mentoring is to transport and build on what we know about mentoring from traditional face-to-face settings into an online environment (Smith & Israel, 2010). In addition to replacing traditional program elements with online versions, e-mentoring program designers use the unique capacities of technological tools to create innovative mentoring practices. However, transporting practices and devising novel solutions is especially difficult because the most effective and efficient designs have not been clearly established for face-to-face programs (McLeskey & Billingsley, 2008). Although a definitive program design is elusive, current studies offer guidance and ignite excitement about how online tools hold promises for successful mentoring (McCombs & Vakili, 2005).

Promise 1: Greater Access for All

Face-to-face mentoring requires a common location, greatly limiting opportunities for beginning teachers to find experts who share their subject area and grade-level focus. For example, Simonsen, Luebeck, and Bice (2009) describe how teachers in certain locations struggle to find qualified mentors:

> In many of the state's rural schools, there is only one teacher at each grade level (or multiple grades) in a given content area.

> The nearest experienced, content knowledgeable mentor may be more than 50 miles away. The problem is only compounded when the unique needs of teachers in specific content areas, such as science and mathematics, are considered. (p. 52)

Digitally savvy mentors with specific subject-area and grade-level expertise are likely to be found through the Internet to support new teachers, particularly where expert mentors are not locally available. When examining teacher attrition in public schools from 1993 to 2003, the "data show that high-poverty, high-minority, urban, and rural public schools have among the highest rates of turnover" (Ingersoll, Merrill, & Stuckey, 2014, p.23). Yet, intensive mentoring programs have shown increases in teacher retention (Darling-Hammond, 2003). E-mentoring has the potential to provide greater resources, ongoing support, and expertise to teachers in locations where resources are fewer and student needs are greater.

Promise 2: Immediate, Convenient, and Sustainable Communication

E-mentoring provides synchronous and asynchronous meetings, allowing mentees to communicate with mentors anytime and anywhere. Research on traditional mentoring shows that novice teachers seek "in-the-moment" advice and feedback. For example, when asked, twenty-two teachers generally agreed that they "get help from those close by" and "go to those who have a schedule that leaves them available when I need them" (Hunt, Powell, Little, & Mike, 2013, p. 102). This type of immediate help is available online, synchronously through Skype or Google chats and asynchronously via email or discussion boards, providing both mentees and mentors with a wide range of available communication options without location and schedule constraints.

A further advantage, freely available online communication tools enable a mentoring relationship to be sustained throughout a career. For example, Baker-Doyle and Yoon (2011) suggest that novice teachers, being part of the Millennial generation, "are able to maintain long-term relationships outside their workplace through technology" (p. 31). Ease of online communication provides the immediacy, convenience, and sustainability that new teachers are seeking and may lead to long-lasting relationships.

Promise 3: Comfort

Surprisingly, many teachers perceive the online environment as less threatening than face-to-face meetings. Beginning teachers may feel more comfortable articulating fears and sharing problems online because the facial reaction of the listener is often not seen and responses are not immediately expected. Consequently, with more detailed descriptions, online mentors are able to offer precise advice. For example, Simonsen, Luebeck, and Bice (2009) found that when online, "beginning teachers can interact with mentors who are far removed from the politics of their own local school building or district. With the comfort provided by distance, they are free to talk safely about frustrations with administrators, colleagues, and parents, seeking the advice of experts or simply venting emotions with no fear of reprisal" (p. 52).

Additionally, e-mentoring may diminish the effects of differences in social status, age, gender, and race in mentoring relationships (Headlam-Wells, Gosland, & Craig, 2005) as physical characteristics are "less visible in electronic communication, thus rendering them less important to the overall exchange" (Bierema & Merriam, 2002, p. 221). Another benefit to connecting with mentors online is that teachers gain the opportunity to learn different perspectives and build on the successes of a wide range of educators from other locations, including other countries (Risser, 2013). Increasing the comfort, precision, and perspectives may lead to more efficient and focused development of teacher expertise.

Promise 4: Personalization

E-mentoring is uniquely situated to adapt to the individual needs and school context of each beginning teacher. With online tools, it is simple for a mentee to filter a discussion board to see only posts that address a specific topic such as parent communication or student behavior. Likewise, mentors can search through example advice posted from other mentors by grade level, subject, problem, or resolution. Both mentee and mentor can register for alerts via email or text when another educator creates a new post on a particular topic.

An e-mentoring system can easily be programmed to use crowd sourcing to recommend to beginning teachers and their mentors the advice and resources that other educators with similar characteristics have used to improve their practice. An Amazon.com approach can be used—for example, "Other third grade teachers who were interested in grading policies also read these posts or downloaded these resources." Therefore, the online experience can be flexibly personalized to each user every time they log into the website, focusing their attention on resources and experts related to the individual's immediate concern or need.

Promise 5: Ongoing Assessment

Mentors can use e-Tools such as written records of interactions and digitized artifacts including video, text, and images to help new teachers reflect on their practices, evaluate the instructional competencies of beginning professionals, and assess the impact of their mentoring. Mentors may set goals with mentees and then use the digital artifacts to monitor progress toward achieving the goals. A digital record enables mentors to track the types of discussions and resources that were necessary to make changes in a teacher's practice.

When online, data on participant behavior are automatically generated during e-mentoring. Tracer data may include information such as time, length of communication, number of responses, and the individual initiating communication or responding to others. These data enable learning analytics to describe the ways participants are interacting with each other and using resources. Computers facilitate data mining by sorting, searching, counting, and archiving posts, emails, and artifacts enabling participants themselves as well as monitors or researchers to begin to understand subjects under discussion and nature of the questions and responses.

Promise 6: Engaging Multimedia

Beginning teachers benefit from observing teaching and collaboratively analyzing instructional practices. Linda Darling-Hammond (2009) reports that "effective teaching strategies cannot be learned merely from reading about them or being told what to do by a mentor" (p. 16). The online environment is particularly useful for sharing videos from classrooms to see practices "in action" and provide a source for careful reflection through slow-motion observations and replaying. This type of viewing can't be done during a live classroom observation. Although webcams in the classroom and videos of beginning teachers can't replicate the experience of classroom coaching during instruction, these tools offer opportunities for reflective coaching and planning that are different and valuable.

Multimedia tools expand far beyond classroom videos; for example, beginning teachers might create a "talk diary" where they simply make an audio recording using their cell phone or an iPad of their reflections on the day's lessons and learning. Tools like *Speech to Text* can turn these audio files into written texts for reading and discussion with other educators or the files can be made into a listening library for examining reflections over time.

Promise 7: Contemporary Literacies—
Conversations from One's Fingertips

Interestingly, the format of contemporary literacies may be particularly suited to encourage deep reflective thinking. Consider the process a mentor or mentee might use to compose and publish a blog describing a question, classroom situation, or implementation of an instructional practice. Bloggers use a complete writing process including drafting, editing, conferencing, revising, and ultimately publishing the blog to a public website. Online visitors offer feedback and the authors may engage in further revision and extension of their thinking.

Gawande (2011) describes the development of expertise as a process that "requires going from unconscious incompetence to conscious incompetence to conscious competence and finally to unconscious competence" (p. 50). The writing process of online communication may facilitate deep reflection that develops expertise. Ironically, although new technology can make communication faster or "instant," the same technology can demand slow reflective thinking and conversations (Wheeler & Lambert-Heggs, 2009).

Promise 8: A Community of Support

E-mentoring provides beginning teachers with opportunities for increased interactions with a larger community and many avenues for participation. "E-mentoring is not necessarily based on a wise elder dispensing advice and instruction to a protégée. Rather it is a mutually beneficial relationship that is highly versatile and can be adapted to work in a variety of settings" (Bierema & Merriam, 2002, p. 219). For example, online discussion boards "have potential for addressing the isolation new teachers experience and have been found to help novice teachers realize that their experiences and challenges are similar to that of their peers in other school settings because mentees may communicate with other mentees as well as their mentors (Smith & Israel, 2010, p. 39).

Relationships made through e-mentoring may be expanded from a single experienced mentor to multiple mentors and may include other new teachers in the same discipline and grade level as well as professionals who work in the field (such as historians, architects, and authors). For example, mentors might repurpose the advice of other mentors by directing a mentee to a conversation between another mentor and mentee posted on a discussion board.

These shared conversations build a collective expertise among participants in a professional community and expand the number of available resources that new teachers can go to for help (Risser, 2013). Therefore the amount of interaction and the number of relationships within an e-mentoring program may be larger than traditional mentoring, including mentee–mentor, mentee–mentee, and mentor–mentor relationships. A new teacher's support may include both a large network of professionals who have differing expertise as well as a frequent close relationship with a single mentor (Bierema & Sharan, 2002).

THE PERILS OF NEW TECHNOLOGIES

On the surface, new technologies seem to make mentoring easy. However, unlimited uses of new tools challenge program designers to stay focused on a specific goal. Determining how to avoid potential pitfalls is an essential step in e-mentoring.

Peril 1: Technology Quickly Changes and Disappears

At odds with the slow process of systematically studying how technology supports can increase positive outcomes of mentoring is the fast paced development and changes that take place in how technology works and what tools are available. By the time an e-mentoring tool is developed, established as a resource among teachers, and ready for research on outcomes, technological changes have made the tool obsolete. This results in hypotheses of the possible promises of e-mentoring, but limited research.

Peril 2: Finding Out What Works

The most effective design for e-mentoring is unknown. Systematic research to examine the results of different programs is needed. However, this research is challenging because the goals and methods of e-mentoring programs vary widely; and, as stated in Peril #1, the technology changes so quickly that before studies can be completed and replicated, a new tool makes recent program methods obsolete. In addition, programs can be blended, using e-mentoring as a component of a face-to-face program so there are many combinations of factors that must be examined.

Peril 3: Losing Local Knowledge

Local knowledge has value. The most consistent finding is that retention within a particular school is higher when a mentor has previous experience working in that school, suggesting that an important part of mentoring may be the provision of school specific knowledge. For example, early career special educators will likely have questions about paperwork and resources for students and families. This knowledge is usually specific to a local school, and an e-mentor may not have the needed knowledge to share (Smith & Israel, 2010). In addition, effective teachers understand and make instructional connections to the cultures of students, their families, and the community that surrounds the school. Online mentors may not be aware of the local cultural capital that a beginning teacher needs to learn.

Peril 4: Non-millennial Expert Mentors and Millennial Protégé Communication

Millenials may experience a digital communication culture clash when interacting with mentors who have mentored in a traditional face-to-face setting. Online interactions can easily lead to miscommunication because the conversation is often missing the visual and audible cues that clarify meaning. Even communication shorthand like "brb" (be right back), "lol" (laugh out loud), and "gtg" (got to go) can lead to confusion among generations. Because communication is the primary activity of mentoring, a significant concern for e-mentoring is the probable miscommunication that yields from interactions that are "asynchronous, primarily text-based, and relatively fast, with participants often widely geographically distributed" (Harris, O'Bryan, & Rotenberg, 1996, p. 55).

Peril 5: Shadowing and Observing in Local Settings

Shadowing and observing master teachers and reflecting together on the expertise seen are critical pieces of many traditional mentoring programs. Mentors provide critical coaching to help teachers apply their learning from observations and analysis to their own planning and teaching in the classroom. Through traditional mentoring, the mentor might visit the beginning teacher's classroom and actually join in teaching to model specific techniques with the students (Schwille, 2008).

This informal, in-the-classroom coaching cannot be accomplished through e-mentoring. Although webcams, Google hangouts, and Skype make real-time observations and conversations possible, the preparation and technology glitches may deter participants from this option. The amount of planning time needed to record a lesson is huge in comparison to simply walking down the hall to observe. However, a great benefit for both mentees and mentors is the ability to record a lesson and then watch the event online together to reflect and discuss. Still, rewatching takes time that may not be available. The informal observation and working together in a classroom often seen between mentee and mentor in traditional mentoring are lost in e-mentoring.

Peril 6: Sustaining Interest and Maintaining an Online Community

Sustaining interest and encouraging mentees and mentors to participate rather than lurking over discussions boards are challenges. Ongoing programs need to build a system of supports for both the mentor and mentees to develop strong relationships that naturally lead to continuous conversations (Kamel Boulos et al., 2006). Some programs address this peril through a facilitator who monitors progress toward the program goals, follows up with mentors as well as mentees, and supplies prompts to keep conversations and relationships active (Bierema & Merriam, 2002).

Peril 7: Time

Lack of time is a constant concern for educators. Unfortunately, "instant" communication doesn't mean that less time is consumed than in traditional conversations. All forms of social media require an investment of time. For example, written online communication such as reflective blogging is often formal, going through the entire writing process before posting to a public website. While this process can lead to deeper reflective practice, it may also require more time than holding a meeting with a mentor during lunchtime.

BEST PRACTICES FOR IMPLEMENTING E-MENTORING

While there is no handbook for designing and launching e-mentoring, features from what we know about effective face-to-face offer guidelines for best practices.

1. Establish Clear Goals, Time Expectations, and Assessment Measures

Whether a formal or informal program is planned, a necessary outcome of mentoring is the rapid acquisition of expertise leading to greater self-efficacy and ultimately increased student achievement (Scherer, 2012). However, small goals may be established with related time frames for a specific mentoring program. For example, an e-mentoring program could be established to support teachers in implementing new discussion techniques related to the Common Core standards. Teachers new to the technique may be assigned a mentor for a semester to provide support through online communication with the implementation of the discussion techniques. Because success is measured by the accomplishment of goals, it is important for both mentors and mentees to understand the purpose of the program and the expected time for accomplishing the goals.

2. Choose Technology and Determine Costs

The technology chosen will determine the "place" where mentoring happens and facilitates how participants engage with each other. Many e-mentoring programs choose a content management system, such as Moodle or Blackboard, to host the interactions. These platforms also provide tools to assess the quantity and quality of the mentoring taking place. Open-source platforms provide free access to the software needed to blog or create a website.

The equipment used in e-mentoring—such as webcams and built-in microphones—is standard in most computers (Israel, Carnahan, Snyder, & Williamson, 2012). Although the technology tools are inexpensive or free, the management and maintenance require human hours that must be considered in the overall costs. The associated human resources and costs related to the implementation of e-mentoring include design, establishment, maintenance, and method of sustaining use of the platform.

3. Recruit and Prepare Mentors

Mentoring is a strategic practice that requires more knowledge and skills than being an expert teacher of students (Fong, Mansor, Zakaria, Sharif, & Nordin, 2012). A mentor must understand the beginning teacher as a learner, the school context, and the immediate need to learn something about teaching. Mentoring must be differentiated based on each individual teacher making it hard for mentors to know exactly what actions are expected. Online training modules, materials, and discussion boards provide mentors with ongoing "anytime / anywhere" preparation and assessment of mentor skills.

4. Match Mentees to Mentors

Pogodzinski (2012) theorized that individuals interact more often and discuss the practice of teaching more frequently in mentoring relationships when the individuals share a high degree of similarities. A database can be used to record both mentee and mentor interests, concerns, and characteristics of the current work context, facilitating matches between mentees to mentors who share many similarities. Matches made through data analysis may have a better instructional fit for mentees than matches made off-line in traditional mentoring using the primary characteristic of location.

5. Set Communication Norms

Teachers from the millennial generation are already in the habit of going online to ask for help and look for resources. New technologies engage educators in speaking, listening, watching, writing, and reading online. This is markedly different than traditional mentoring completed primarily through informal conversations. Because these tools are so new, it is essential that mentoring programs establish explicit norms for communication among participants in the community. These norms may include expectations for participation, response time, language use, a clear process for offering feedback, and guidelines for disagreeing online.

The norms may also define and encourage participants to be active in a range of ways, from posting and replying to others to simply reading posts but not responding. Finally, norms that help participants know how to end relationships are also important so that participants don't simply vanish from discussions. Communication expectations and norms for learning together are critical to e-mentoring program success.

EXAMPLE PRACTICES: DO-IT-ONESELF MENTORING WITH WEB 2.0 TOOLS

With e-mentoring, there is no reason that beginning teachers can't have pedagogical and content specific support using mentors from both down the hallway and all around the globe. Whether part of a formal e-mentoring program or informally used by an individual, Web 2.0 tools can increase reflective practice and the development of instructional expertise. For example, to deepen reflective practice, many new teachers are blogging as a vehicle for reflection, feedback, and collaboration. These blogs serve an informal mentoring process and are uniquely valuable for reflection because the archive feature shows a history of posts listed chronologically. Other beginning teachers may benefit from reading another's experience through these blogs. Both mentors and new teachers alike may leave comments or engage in a discussion prompted by the blog.

Amazingly, a complete informal e-mentoring program could be custom made by new teachers for themselves using the freely available tools and online communities. Tools such as Google chat, Skype, videoconferencing, Twitterchat, discussion boards, wikis, blogs, instant messaging, and text messaging can facilitate the process of mentoring. For example, beginning teachers and expert mentors can sign up for mentoring matches using a Google Doc at the *New Teacher Mentoring Project*. Mentees sign up and then search the Google Doc to find mentors with the expertise that is sought. Or new teachers can join the new teacher chat on Twitter to find a network of experts and beginning teachers to help (https://twitter.com/hashtag/#ntchat).

Resources can be found on YouTube channels, such as Edutopia's New-Teacher Academy. These short, easily accessible videos provide new teachers with needed knowledge and examples of instructional practices in action that can be accessed anytime every day. In addition, there are freely accessible videos to train mentors, such as Educational Impact's "Mentoring & Coaching: The Journey of a First-Year Teacher."

Clearly, every element of a formal mentoring program—from matching mentors to mentees, training mentors, and holding meetings—is available informally to anyone with access to the Internet who chooses to participate. The available tools create a "Do-It-Yourself" opportunity, where beginning teachers are able to create a mentoring program that suits their specific needs. E-mentoring is more than an online program—it can be used as a network of resources for collaboration that are available to teachers for professional learning throughout their careers.

Is Instant Mentoring Better?

Research establishes that mentoring plays an important role in developing teacher expertise, including many positive results such as increased self-efficacy, retention rates, and student achievement (Darling-Hammond, 2013). In fact, Villar (2009) evaluated an e-mentoring program and found that the retention rate was 80–95 percent for participants, comparable to similar face-to-face programs. In addition, student achievement in both reading and math improved when teachers received more hours of mentoring, offering support that mentoring positively impacts teaching skills and related student achievement (Rockoff, 2008).

Opportunities are abundant for new types of e-mentoring as available technology changes the way people build relationships, access information, and communicate, providing greater support for all teachers. However, in the end, technology serves only as the method and means for e-mentoring. Similar to traditional mentoring programs, the keys to e-mentoring success are the actual relationships built that effectively develop expertise and improve learning outcomes for students (Rockwell, Leck, & Elliott, 2013). The many promises and perils of new technologies can overwhelm program designers. However, by focusing on the use of technologies that facilitate achieving specific program goals and those that support the key components of mentoring, building relationships, and fostering effective communication, e-mentoring may change the time and resources needed to provide sustained help to all beginning teachers everywhere and to continue that support throughout their careers.

RESOURCES DISCUSSED

Google Docs https://support.google.com/docs/answer/49008?hl=en
Skype http://www.skype.com/en/about/
Moodle https://moodle.org/
Blackboard http://www.blackboard.com/
Weebly http://www.weebly.com/
Blogger https://www.blogger.com/features
WordPress http://wordpress.com
New Teacher Mentoring Project http://www.lisadabbs.com/new-teacher-mentoring-project
New Teacher Chat Twitter https://twitter.com/hashtag/#ntchat
Edutopia's New-Teacher Academy: The First Year Experience http://www.edutopia.org/blog/new-teacher-lesson-planning-lisa-dabbs
Mentoring & Coaching: The Journey of a First Year Teacher https://www.youtube.com/watch?v=5hrqMwEyfn0

REFERENCES

Baker-Doyle, K. J., & Yoon, S. A. (2011). In search of practitioner-based social capital: A social network analysis tool for understanding and facilitating teacher collaboration in a US-based STEM professional development program. *Professional development in Education, 37*(1), 75–93.

Bierema, L. L. M., & Merriam, S. B. (2002). E-mentoring: Using Computer Mediated Communication to Enhance the Mentoring Process. *Innovative Higher Education, 26*(3), 211–227.

Darling-Hammond, L. (2003). Keeping good teachers: Why it matters, what leaders can do. *Educational Leadership, 60*(8), 6–13.

———. (2009). A future worthy of teaching for America. *Education Digest, 74*(6), 11–16.

———. (2013). When teachers support & evaluate their peers. *Educational Leadership, 71*(2), 24–29.

Darling-Hammond, L. (2003). Keeping good teachers: Why it matters, what leaders can do. *Educational Leadership, 60*(8), 6–13.

Fong, N. S., Mansor, W. F. A. W., Zakaria, M. H., Sharif, N. H. M., & Nordin, N. A. (2012). The Roles of mentors in a collaborative virtual learning environment (CVLE) project. *Procedia: Social and Behavioral Sciences, 66*, 302–311. doi:10.1016/j.sbspro.2012.11.272.

Gawande, A. (October 3, 2011). Personal best. *The New Yorker*, 3, 44–53. http://www.newyorker.com/reporting/2011/10/03/111003fa_fact_gawande?currentPage=all

Harris, J., O'Bryan, E., & Rotenberg, L. (1996). Practical lessons in telementoring. *Learning and Leading with Technology, 24* (2), 53–57.

Headlam-Wells, J., Gosland, J., & Craig, J. (2005). "There's magic in the web": E-mentoring for women's career development. *Career Development International, 10*(6), 444–459.

Hunt, J. H., Powell, S., Little, M. E., & Mike, A. (2013). The Effects of E-Mentoring on Beginning Teacher Competencies and Perceptions. *Teacher Education and Special Education: The Journal of the Teacher Education Division of the Council for Exceptional Children, 36*(4), 286–297. doi:10.1177/0888406413502734.

Ingersoll, R. M., & Strong, M. (2011). The impact of induction and mentoring programs for beginning teachers: A critical review of the research. *Review of Educational Research, 81*(2), 201–233.

Ingersoll, R., Merrill, L., & Stuckey, D. (April, 2014). *Seven trends: The transformation of the teaching force*. Philadelphia, PA: Consortium for Policy Research in Education.

Israel, M., Carnahan, C. R., Snyder, K. K., & Williamson, P. (2012). Supporting new teachers of students with significant disabilities through virtual coaching: A proposed model. *Remedial & Special Education, 34*(4), 195–204. doi:10.1177/0741932512450517.

McCombs, B. L., & Vakili, D. (2005). A learner-centered framework for E-learning. *Teachers College Record, 107*(8), 1582–1600. doi:10.1111/j.1467-9620.2005.00534.x.

McLeskey, J., & Billingsley, B. S. (2008). How does the quality and stability of the teaching force influence the research-to-practice gap? A perspective on the teacher shortage in special education. *Remedial and Special Education, 29*(5), 293–305.

Pogodzinski, B. (2012). Considering the social context of schools: A framework for investigating new teacher induction. *Mentoring & Tutoring: Partnership in Learning, 20*(3), 325–342.

Risser, H. (2013). Virtual induction: A novice teacher's use of Twitter to form an informal mentoring network. *Teaching and Teacher Education*, 3525–3533. doi:10.1016/j.tate.2013.05.001.

Rockoff, J. E. (2008). *Does Mentoring Reduce Turnover and Improve Skills of New Employees? Evidence from Teachers in New York City* (Working Paper No. 13868). National Bureau of Economic Research. Retrieved from http://www.nber.org/papers/w13868.

Rockwell, B. V., Leck, J. D., & Elliott, C. J. (2013). Can e-mentoring take the "gender" out of mentoring? *Cyberpsychology: Journal of Psychosocial Research on Cyberspace, 7*(2), article 5. doi: 10.5817/CP2013-2-5.

Scherer, M. (2012). The challenges of supporting new teachers. *Educational Leadership, 69*(8), 18–23.

Schwille, S. A. (2008). The professional practice of mentoring. *American Journal of Education, 115*(1), 139–167. doi:10.1086/590678.

Simonsen, L., Luebeck, J., & Bice, L. (2009). The effectiveness of Online Paired Mentoring for beginning science and mathematics teachers. *International Journal of E-Learning & Distance Education, 23*(2), 51–68.

Smith, S. J., & Israel, M. (2010). E-mentoring: Enhancing special education teacher induction. *Journal of Special Education Leadership, 23*(1), 30–40.

Villar, A. (2009). *eMSS Mentoring and Retention Survey: Final Report*. University of California, Santa Cruz.

Wheeler, S., & Lambert-Heggs, W. (2009). Connecting distance learners and their mentors using blogs: The mentorBlog project. *Quarterly Review of Distance Education, 10*(4), 323–331.

Chapter Nine

Preparing Women to Lead

Relating Mentoring to Success

Deirdre Callahan

> For all the nameless women whose work has been overlooked, and for those endangered women who set things in motion and bring about change but who must remain nameless. (*1000 Peacewomen Across the Globe*, 2006)

The American Association of School Administrators released its *AASA 2010 Decennial Study of Superintendents* (Kowalski, McCord, Petersen, Young, & Ellerson, 2011), a follow-up to the *2000 Study of the American Superintendency* (Glass, Bjork, Brunner, Brunner, & Glass, 2001). The results revealed that although there was an increase in the number of women superintendents (from 13.2 percent in 2000 to 24.1 percent in 2010), this figure is still impressively lower than the finding that 75 percent of superintendents are men.

Grogan and Shakeshaft (2011) note that "women still do not fill administrative positions in proportion to their numbers in teaching, or in proportion to those who are now trained and certified to become administrators" (p. 28). Within this context, the question that we need to continue to ask is why is this so—are women either not interested in or unable to obtain a senior-level position in the field they dominate, in this instance the superintendency—and what can we do about it?

MENTORING AND WOMEN'S CAREER SUCCESS

Studies of women in leadership positions and related issues suggest that support and mentoring can play a large role for women who are serving or want to serve in leadership positions in the field of education (Dunbar & Kinnnersley, 2011; Kamler, 2006; LaForrest & Wilson-Jones, 2010; Mendez-Morse, 2004; Rosenberg, 2013). Based on her research on women superintendents in Georgia, Copeland (2013) found that they "preferred a female mentor in part due to their increased understanding of the challenges faced by women in the superintendency" (p. 139). The women superintendents in her study claimed the following:

> [that they] benefitted from mentoring and their experiences had been exceedingly positive . . . [that] women aspiring to the field would benefit by having a female mentor guide and support . . . guidance from experienced superintendents had assisted them with many issues. (Copeland, 2013, p. 142)

According to Washington (2010), "One of the main barriers women face when trying to climb the career ladder is limited access to mentoring and/or less effective mentoring than male counterparts" (p. 12). Although she did not find a difference between the effects of style of mentoring, she did find that being mentored by a white male can be very effective, more so than having a female mentor. Washington noted that although the benefits of mentoring have become widely understood and accepted as well as perceived of as a very important career development tool, many professionals, especially women, never have had the opportunity to be mentored.

Hazel Marsicano, author of the seminal 1981 article "Role of Mentors in Developing Careers: Do Women Need Mentors?" believed that lack of adequate role models and mentors was a great obstacle to women's career advancement and realization of their potential.

IN AN EMBARRASSMENT OF RICHES, WHERE ARE ALL THE FEMALE LEADERS?

A Case of the Glass Ceiling

The glass-ceiling aphorism has served as the stock explanation for the lack of women in leadership and positions of power in politics, business, and education across America (Rapp, Silent, & Silent, 2001). Former Secretary of State Hillary Rodham Clinton referenced the metaphor in a recent interview on her possible run for the presidency: "I'm certainly in the camp that says we need to break down that highest, hardest glass ceiling in American politics" (Vagianos, 2014, p. 11). The glass ceiling continues to be a deterrent to women's leadership even as we have entered the twenty-first century. In their 2006 book *Women in the Superintendency: Discarded Leadership,* Dana and Bourisaw note that the glass ceiling still exists when they address the small percentage of women superintendents in public schools. More recently, LaForrest and Wilson-Jones (2010) wrote that

> as we advance into the 21st century . . . although there is a significant growth of women in the educational profession, the growth is not indicated in the increase of women in senior level leadership positions. Despite some growth, women still must

> learn to function in a male dominated leadership culture, and it becomes difficult for many women to break through and succeed against the glass ceiling. (pp. 2–3)

Hoff and Mitchell (2008), addressing gender discrimination at the education leadership level, report that although the demand for education leaders is pressing,

> women remain underrepresented in leadership roles, particularly in high school principalships and superintendencies, the positions that carry the most responsibility and influence and highest salaries. . . . Numerous scholars have argued that gender-related factors often deter women from entering school administrative roles and impede their progress toward advancement. (Introduction section, para. 2)

They stress that the problem lies with society's polarized gender norms for men and women. For example, males are viewed as strong and assertive, women as fragile and passive. Thus, when men in leadership positions are authoritative, it is seen as an asset. On the other hand, when women leaders engage in the same behavior, they are viewed as being too assertive, which is not considered a positive female trait. Thus, women leaders tend to experience a high degree of stress when they try to meet both leadership expectations and female role expectations. Reporting on the key themes that emerged from their study on educational leaders, Hoff and Mitchell (2008) summarized them as follows:

1. Regarding how the men and women perceived the situation, a large number of both sexes denied that gender was a factor in obtaining leadership. Rather, they claimed that it was based on the individual's credentials and abilities. Thus, "meritoc-

racy" was what both men and women believed was the key factor that played a role in leadership success. (para. 44)

2. Although administrative leadership in schools remains "patriarchal" both visibly as well as in a "nuanced" manner, once again, both men (79 percent) and women (51 percent) believed that gender did not play a role in "advancement." (para. 45)

3. Women reported that they felt they had to be "super-prepared" even when encouraged to apply for a leadership role or for advancement. (para. 46)

4. Both men and women conceded that leadership qualities are still viewed as more consistent with male rather than female traits. Women remarked that this attitude made their community relationships difficult, unlike the men, who did not report a similar problem (para. 4)

Ban Bossy

Sheryl Sandberg (2013), author of the national best seller *Lean In: Women, Work, and the Will to Lead*, pointed to gender bias in the workplace as a factor that makes it harder for women to get leadership positions. She advocated that one needs to start at a young age to help females (and males) overcome the bias that works against females. In an interview with Cynthia McFadden (McFadden & Whitman, 2014), co-anchor of the ABC program *Nightline*, Sandberg talked about younger children because she believes that female difficulty with leadership starts at a young age. Sandberg felt so strongly about this that she launched "a public service campaign called 'Ban Bossy'," working with such notable female leaders as "former Secretary of State Condoleezza Rice and Girl Scouts USA

CEO Anna Maria Chávez" (para. 5). On the Ban Bossy website, Sandberg remarks that

> when a little boy asserts himself, he's called a "leader." Yet when a little girl does the same, she risks being branded "bossy." Words like bossy send a message: don't raise your hand or speak up. By middle school, girls are less interested in leading than boys—a trend that continues into adulthood. (2014, p. 1)

According to McFadden, Sandberg remarked that "we call them [girls] too aggressive or other B-words in the workplace. They're bossy as little girls, and then they're aggressive, political, shrill, too ambitious as women" (para. 4). The campaign's goal assists females at all ages to "feel more confident and comfortable as leaders" (para. 9). Sandberg viewed it as critical that females (and males) must be taught to understand that "leadership is not bullying and leadership is not aggression . . . [it] is the expectation that you can use your voice for good" (para. 14).

GENDER ROLES: EMOTIONAL AND EMPATHETIC OR DOMINANT AND FOCUSED?

Differences in men and women's leadership styles and why they are or might be different have drawn much attention, as is the issue of whether they are merely perceived as differing. In a recent article, "Management of Gender Roles: Marketing the Androgynous Leadership Style in the Classroom and the General Workplace," Way and Marques (2013) revive an older construct, "androgyny," that played a major, albeit disputed, role in the early days of the feminist movement during the 1960s and 1970s (see Bem, 1974, 1976; Heilbrun, 1973).

Way and Marques (2013) defined *androgyny* as "the state or condition of having a high degree of both feminine and masculine traits" (p. 83). They noted that "successful leaders most often have an androgynous balance of traits that includes gregariousness, positive initiative and assertion, social skills, intelligence, conscientiousness, integrity, trustworthiness, and the ability to persuade, inspire, and motivate others" (p. 85).

In the Way and Marques (2013) study of forty-eight participants who had worked for at least three years, they found that all respondents supported the notion of androgynous leadership. This was reflected in their perceptions of how male and female leaders could improve. "Male leaders were considered in need of communication, empathy, adaptation, connection, trust, patience, and organizing . . . need for more sensitivity" (p. 90). Female leaders were seen as being "too emotional, and too focused on proving themselves" (p. 90).

Friends in High Places: The Old Boys' Club

In addition to a societal bias in favor of male styles of leadership, Ortiz criticizes educational organizations for not guiding men, women, and minorities equally toward leadership, with white males "reaping the most benefits from organizational support" (as cited in Kamler, 2006, p. 1). Myung, Loeb, and Horng (2011) explored the extent to which female principals, when they were teachers, had been encouraged by their principals to become administrators. Although a vast majority of the women superintendents reported that they had been tapped by their own principal when they were teachers, they also noted that principals tended to do so more often with males and those of the same ethnicity as the principal.

The August 2011 issue of the Cato Institute's *New Girl Order: Are Men in Decline?* includes an article, "Co-Opt the Old Boys' Club: Make It Work for Women," by Ilene Lang (2011). She was former CEO and president of Catalyst, a renowned and leading nonprofit organization, dedicated to "expanding opportunities for women and business." Lang writes that the old boys' club "is alive and well because it works. In elite circles, decisions are made behind closed doors. Certain candidates bypass others because of close connections with advocates" (para. 4).

Lang (2011) cites the Urban Dictionary's definition of the old boys' network, because she finds it "frank yet accurate," as follows:

> It is not necessarily purposeful or malicious, but . . . it entails establishing business relationships on high-priced golf courses, at exclusive country clubs, in the executive sky-boxes at sporting events . . . arenas from which women and minorities are traditionally excluded and thus are not privy to the truly "serious" business transactions or conversations. (para. 3)

In the same Cato Institute issue, *New Girl Order: Are Men in Decline?* Hess (2011) notes:

> Female students have mentors, too, but they're less likely to be CEOs or senior executives. . . . Why? Because men mentor men and women mentor women. . . . This is how the glass ceiling is built: Even women who enter the workforce head-to-head with their male peers are less likely to be extended a hand to climb to the upper echelon. (paras. 6–7)

Gender Bias and Stereotyping in Women's Careers— Still Alive, Well, and Kicking

Pirouznia (2013) suggested that the continued existence of gender bias and stereotyping against women at the administrative level in educational systems needs to be brought out into the open and shared with others, both within and outside the school system, if one is to be constructively able to diminish or eradicate its role. She believes that male characteristics are preferred over those of women for leadership "perhaps because people are not aware, nor have experienced, alternative forms of leadership" (p. 308).

Slattery (2006) asserts that when women occupy positions of power, such as the superintendency, it is viewed as gender nonconformity and can result in reprisal and backlash for them. However, very little has been written about the choices women make when constructing their careers. Furthermore, when women do obtain supervisory roles in education, they too often try to imitate the more traditional "male styles" of leadership that they have experienced all their lives, and they are often unsuccessful.

McCrea and Ehrich (2000) reinforce these views. They suggest that the "gendering" of organizations is what creates barriers for women." Traditionally organizational cultures can be described as masculine, which results in the valuing of male qualities and female traits being "devalued or ignored" (para. 1). They add that "at its extreme, a masculinist view of leadership is authoritarian and hierarchical as well as competitive and unemotional" (para. 2).

The Elephant in the Room

But what of female leaders themselves? Or, as Brunner and Kim (2010) put it in the title of their article, "Are Women Prepared to Be Superintendents? Myths and Misunderstandings." Are the few women who have achieved positions of leadership and responsibility stepping up to help female colleagues in the same numbers as their male counterparts? Or is there a tendency for female leaders to disassociate themselves from other women out of a misplaced fear of catering to negative stereotypes? Does a lack of women's mutual, collegial help actually reduce the number of women participating in school leadership? In "Breaking the Gender Barrier," Root (2010) provided some valuable insights into females' perceptions and behaviors and about where women stand on some of these issues. Her primary thrust in this article was on emphasizing how women have the choice of whether they will rise above the notion that gender is an obstacle to their careers. In her words:

> The real issue of *inequality* or gender, or men versus women, lies in the perception individual's hold of themselves, and their understanding of the world around them. What is relevant is that the individual . . . perceives that what she is capable of is of equal benefit to herself and her career, and that she is responsible for what she produces. It is my argument, that what would be a very convenient excuse for women, gender inequality, . . . is really not the *pink elephant* in the room. (p. 1)

Whoever Has Power Takes Over the Noun—and the Norm

Jacques Derrida emphasized the pervasive idea in Western culture that there must be a center, or a truth (as cited in Thurer, 2005), and the philosophy using the Western practice of "privileging" one group against the other, such as in white and black, or, in this case, male and female. When opposites exist, one must be deemed to be better or more powerful, or valued more highly than the other. Carol Gilligan, author of the highly acclaimed book *In a Different Voice* (1982), which had momentous impact when it first came out and continues to do so, focused on how women think and speak with "a different voice" than do men.

Her work supports Derrida's views to a large extent. She based her work within the framework of communication theory as well as the theory of moral development. Her major thesis was that when confronted with moral issues, men and women speak differently, so that whereas females view it from their ethic of care, men base their views on an ethic of justice. It is clear how this distinction between men and women plays a role in the leadership issue.

In a recent 2011 publication, "Looking Back to Look Forward: Revisiting in a Different Voice," thirty years after her book was published, Gilligan argues that the title, *In a Different Voice*,

> calls for a new way of speaking, a change in the very terms of the conversation about ourselves and morality, women and men—about the human condition. Psychologists had assumed a culture in which men were the measure of humanity, and autonomy and rationality ("masculine" qualities) were the markers of maturity. It was a culture that counted on women not speaking for themselves. (para. 3)

So, in the same way that Derrida spoke of society tending to provide privilege to one group over the other, Gilligan shows how morality plays a role in the different voices of men and women, "not in the usual sense of establishing right and wrong, good and bad, but by enforcing women's silence in the name of goodness" (para. 7). She emphasizes that

> I cannot go further in talking about gender . . . without speaking about its relation to patriarchy, an order of living based upon gender: where being a man means not being a woman and also being on top (para. 10). . . . Within a *patriarchal* framework,

care is a feminine ethic. Within a *democratic* framework, care is a human ethic. (para. 17)

If gender is constructed, then it can be deconstructed, which Thurer (2005) analogizes to "de-boning" a fish. Thurer once again refers to Derrida, who advocated that to look into the depths of a language's biases, the language should be deconstructed to rid it of the tendency of structuralism, which is based largely on the oppositions of categories. Derrida thought it important to deconstruct all distinctions or binaries. Thus, deconstruction, when applied to gender, would involve reassembling notions of and language related to gender and gender roles and differences in all areas, as well as in the realm of educational leadership.

CONCLUSION

Mentoring and support for women in the educational system are critical if women are to be able to fulfill their potential and play a more vital role as leaders and administrators. Society in the United States has come a long way toward recognizing the dangers of gender bias and stereotyping that has traditionally made it more difficult for women to achieve their goals. But, these are not yet absent from our society and its institutions. For this reason, women are more in need of being helped to see that the "world is their oyster" and to be shown how they can succeed despite ongoing biases.

At the same time, women need to be assured that gender, in and of itself, is not necessarily the only issue that hinders their career progress. Rather, women have to be helped to view themselves as individuals who can escape the gender role restrictions that exist around them if they choose to do so.

It seems appropriate to conclude this discussion on preparing women to lead with a quote from Gilligan's 2011 article, "Looking Back to Look Forward: Revisiting in a Different Voice," in which she explains:

> In writing *In a Different Voice*, I became starkly aware that if I listened to the voices of women I would be challenging the voices of authority. If women's voices differ . . . there was . . . a need for a different voice . . . a world where it was necessary for a woman to learn to think in a way that differed from the way she really thought if she wanted to be heard and understood. (para. 61)

Looking forward then, we can expect a struggle. As long as the different voice sounds different, the tensions between democracy and patriarchy continue. (para. 64)

REFERENCES

1000 Women for the Nobel Peace Prize Association. (2005). *1000 peacewomen across the globe*. Zurich: Scalo.

Bem, S. L. (1974). The measurement of psychological androgyny. *Journal of Consulting and Clinical Psychology, 42,* 155–162.

———. (1976). Sex typing and androgyny: Further explorations of the expressive domain. *Journal of Personality and Social Psychology, 34,* 1016.

Brunner, C. C., & Kim, Y. (2010). Are women prepared to be superintendents? Myths and misunderstandings. *Journal of Research on Leadership Education, 5*(8), 276–309.

Clifford, J. L. (2014). *The perceptions and experiences of women working as teachers at the secondary level who hold administrative licenses but who do not work as administrators*. Education Doctoral Theses. Paper 171. Retrieved from http://hdl.handle.net/2047/d20004955

Coleman, M. (2003). Gender and the orthodoxies of leadership. *School Leadership & Management, 23,* 325–339.

Copeland, S. (2013). *Perceptions of mentoring: Examining the experiences of women superintendents in Georgia* (Unpublished doctoral dissertation). Georgia Southern University, Statesboro, GA. Retrieved from http://

digitalcommons.georgiasouthern.edu/cgi/viewcontent.cgi?article=1921&context=etd

Dana, J. A., & Bourisaw, D. M. (2006). *Women in the superintendency: Discarded leadership.* Lanham, MD: Rowman & Littlefield Education.

Dunbar, D. R., & Kinnersley, R. T. (2011). Mentoring female administrators toward leadership success. *Delta Kappa Gamma Bulletin, 77*(3), 17–24.

Gates, S. M., Ringel, J. S., & Santibanez, L., with Chung, C. H., & Ross, K. E. (2003). *Who is leading our schools? An overview of school administrators and their careers.* Santa Monica, CA: Rand Corporation. Retrieved from http://www.rand.org/pubs/monograph_reports/MR1679.html

Gilligan, C. (1982). *In a different voice.* Cambridge, MA: Harvard University Press.

Gilligan, C. (2011). Looking back to look forward: Revisiting in a different voice. *Classics, Issue 9, Defense Mechanisms.* Retrieved from http://chs.harvard.edu/wa/pageR?tn=ArticleWrapper&bdc=12&mn=4025

Glass, T. E., Bjork, L., Brunner, C. C., Brunner, C. C., & Glass, T. (2001). *2000 study of the American superintendency.* Alexandria, VA: American Association of School Administrators.

Grogan, M., & Shakeshaft, C. (2011). *Women and educational leadership.* San Francisco, CA: Jossey-Bass.

Heilbrun, C. G. (1973). *Toward a recognition of androgyny.* New York: Alfred A. Knopf.

Hess, A. (2011, August 12). The old boys' club lives on. *Cato Unbound. A Journal of Debate.* Retrieved from http://www.cato-unbound.org/2011/08/12/amanda-hess/old-boys-club-lives

Hoff, D. L., & Mitchell, S. N. (2008). *In search of leaders: Gender discrimination in school administration.* Paper presentation at the National Education Law Conference, July 24–27, Portland, ME.

Kamler, E. (2006). The aspiring superintendents' study group: Investigating a mentoring network for school leaders. *Mentoring & Tutoring, 14,* 297–316.

Kim, Y., & Brunner, C. C. (2009). School administrators' career mobility to the superintendency: Gender differences in career development. *The Journal of Educational Administration, 47*(1), 75–107.

Kowalski, T. J., McCord, R. S., Petersen, G. J., Young, P., & Ellerson, N. M. (2011). *The American school superintendent: 2010 decennial study.* Alexandria, VA: American Association of School Administrators in partnership with Rowman & Littlefield.

LaForrest, L., & Wilson-Jones, L. (2010). Women superintendents: Challenges, barriers and experiences as senior level leaders. *National Forum of Educational Administration and Supervision Journal, 27*(4), 1–7. Retrieved from http://

www.nationalforum.com/Electronic%20Journal%20Volumes/Lane-Washington,%20LaForrest%20Women%20Superintendents%20NFEASJ%20V27%20N4%202010.pdf

Lang, I. H. (2011, November). Co-Opt the Old Boys' Club: Make It Work for Women. *Harvard Business Review*. Retrieved from http://hbr.org/2011/11/co-opt-the-old-boys-club-make-it-work-for-women/ar/1

Marsicano, H. E. (1981. March 28). *Role of mentors in developing careers: Do women need mentors?* Paper presented at the West Virginia University Council on Women's Career Management: Challenge and Decisions. Morgantown, WV.

McCrea, N. L., & Ehrich, L. C. (2000). Completing an educational leadership picture: Feminine essentials from an Australian perspective. In A. Pankake, G. Schroth, & C. Funk (Eds.), *Women as school executives: The complete picture* (pp. 48–54). Commerce, TX: Texas A&M University, Commerce Press.

McFadden, C., & Whitman, J. (2014, March 10). Sheryl Sandberg launches "ban bossy" campaign to empower girls to lead. Retrieved from http://abcnews.go.com/us/sheryl-sandberg-launches-ban-bossy-campaign-empower-girls/story?id=22819181

Mendez-Morse, S. (2004). Constructing mentors: Latina educational leaders' role models and mentors. *Educational Administration Quarterly, 40*, 561–590.

Michigan Association of School Administrators (MASA). (2011, January 1). *10-Year Study on the American School Superintendent Released* [Press release]. Retrieved from http://gomasa.org/news/10-year-study-american-school-superintendent-released

Murphey, K., Moss, G., Hannah, S., & Wiener, R. (2005, January 1). Women in educational leadership: Finding common ground. *Journal of Women in Educational Leadership, 3*(4), 273–284. Retrieved from http://commons.pacificu.edu/cgi/viewcontent.cgi?article1003&context=edufac

Myung, J., Loeb, S., & Horng, E. (2011). Tapping the principal pipeline: Identifying talent for future school leadership in the absence of formal succession management programs. *Education Administration Quarterly, 47*(5), 695–727.

Pirouznia, M. (2013). Voices of Ohio women aspiring to principalship. *Journal of International Women's Studies, 14*(1), 300–310. Retrieved from http://vc.bridgew.edu/cgi/viewcontent.cgi?article=1665&context=jiws

Rapp, D., Silent, X., & Silent, Y. (2001). The implications of raising one's voice in educational leadership doctoral programs: Women's stories of fear, retaliation, and silence. *Journal of School Leadership, 11*(4), 279–295.

Root, R. L. (2010). Breaking the gender barrier. *Forum on Public Policy*. Retrieved http://forumonpublicpolicy.com/spring2010.vol2010/spring2010archive/root.rev.pdf

Rosenberg, M. (2013, April 29). Leaning in? Women superintendents making mark in public education [by Merri Rosenberg On Board Online. The New York State School Boards Association]. Retrieved from http://www.nyssba.org/news/2013/04/26/on-board-online-april-29-2013/leaning-in-women-superintendents-making-mark-in-public-education/

Salon, R. (2011, February 19). *AASA study reveals current facets of superintendency.* Paper presented at the Annual Conference of the The American Association of School Administrators, Nashville, TN. Retrieved from http://www.aasa.org/content.aspx?id=18176

Sandberg, S. (2013). *Lean in: Women, work, and the will to lead.* New York: Knopf.

Skrla, L. (2000). Mourning silence: Women superintendents (and a researcher) rethink speaking up and speaking out. *Qualitative Studies in Education, 13,* 611–628.

Slattery, P. (2006). Curriculum Development in the Postmodern Era (Rev. ed.). New York: Routledge.

Thurer, S. L. (2005). *The end of gender: A psychological autopsy.* New York: Routledge.

Vagianos, A. (2014, June 5). Hillary Clinton says it's time to shatter the "highest, hardest glass ceiling." *The Huffington Post.* Retrieved from http://www.huffingtonpost.com/2014/06/05/hilary-clinton-people-magazine-interview_n_5452564.html

Ward, K., & Eddy, P. L. (2013, December 9). Women and academic leadership: Leaning out. *The Chronicle of Higher Education.* Retrieved from http://chronicle.com/article/WomenAcademic-Leadership-/143503/

Washington, C. E. (2010, Spring). Mentoring, organizational rank, and women's perceptions of advancement opportunities in the workplace. *Forum on Public Policy.* Retreived from http://forumonpublicpolicy.com/spring2010.vol2010/spring2010archive/washington.pdf

Way, A. D., & Marques, J. (2013). Management of gender roles: Marketing the androgynous leadership style in the classroom and the general workplace. *Organization Development Journal, 31*(2), 82–94. Retrieved from http://www.hpu.edu/docs/ohana/OD-Journal-Summer2013.pdf

Young, M. D., & Skrla, L. (Eds.). (2003). *Reconsidering feminist research in educational leadership.* Albany, NY: State University of New York Press.

Index

AASA 2010 Decennial Study of Superintendents (Kowalski, McCord, Petersen, Young and Ellerson), 149
academic expectations, 15–16
academic mentoring: boundaries in, 115; collaborative relationships in, 115, 124–125; defined, 113–114; effective leadership in, 122–123; ethical behavior instilled in, 123; leadership aspects of, 114–115; leadership's benefits for, 119–122; leadership's role in, 117–118; principles of effective, 116, 117–118, 124–125; transformational leadership in, 118–119, 119–121, 121–122, 122–123. *See also* assistant professors; international graduate and doctoral students
access, to e-mentoring, 130–131
accountability: Common Core standards of, 86; cultures of, 90–91, 95–96, 103; for mentor effectiveness, 39, 43, 44; of teachers, 85, 86. *See also* evaluations
Acheson, 106
administration: teacher evaluations by, 86, 89, 108–109; women in, 149–150. *See also* principals; superintendents
adult learning, 13, 17; SDL in, 20–22, 26–28, 27, 28, 29; TL in, 20, 22–23, 26, 27, 28, 29
advancement through advisement, ix
advocacy, 72–73

AERA. *See* American Educational Research Association
Ainsworth, M. S., 6
American Association of School Administrators (ASSA), 149
American Educational Research Association (AERA), 72
Anderson, B., 25
Anderson, E., 116
Anderson, S., 25
androgynous leadership, 154–155
Anfara, V., 37–38
Annenberg Institute, 105
approaches, to mentoring, 4; contemporary, 7–8; developmental process, 5, 10; effective qualities in, 7; in matching mentors and mentees, 4, 10; mentor and mentee relationships in, 6–7
"Are Women Prepared to Be Superintendents? Myths and Misunderstandings" (Brunner and Kim), 157–158
ASSA. *See* American Association of School Administrators
assessments, in e-mentoring, 133–134, 140–141
assistant professors, mentoring of, 70; caring in, 69, 70, 79–80; collegiality and support in, 71–72; communication in, 69, 70, 78; focus and political savvy

165

in, 74; formal mentoring of, 80, 80–81; honesty and advocacy in, 72–73; informal mentoring in, 71, 80, 81; opportunities and exposure in, 75–76; personal reflections on, 71–77, 80–81; publications and personal connection in, 76–77; relationships in, 69, 70, 78–79, 81
attachment theory, 6
Atuahene-Gima, K., 119–120

Baker-Doyle, K. J., 132
Bambino, D., 104
Ban Bossy campaign, 153–154
barriers: gendering of organizations as, 157; language, 18; in relationships, 6, 10
Bass, B. M., 117
Beachum, F. D., 78, 80
"Being the Boss is Hard" (Ginsberg), 38
Berk, R., 119
best practices, for e-mentoring, 140–142
Bezzina, M., 120
bias: gender, 152–153, 157–160, 160; language, 153–154, 160; privilege and, 158, 159
Bice, L., 130–131, 132
blogging, 129, 135, 140, 141, 143
Bolkan, S., 123
boundaries, 115
Bourisaw, D. M., 151
"Breaking the Gender Barrier" (Root), 158
Brockett, R. G., 21
Brown, K., 37–38, 121
Brown, S., 86, 87, 99, 103
Brunner, C. C., 9, 157–158
Burns, J. M., 120
Butcher, J., 120

calendar of new teacher mentoring, 55–56
Capasso, 41
Carducci, R., 118
caring, 69, 70, 79–80
caring communities, 95
Carlson, D., 123
Catholic School Leadership Program, 60–61, 63–64
Catholic school mentoring: Christian education in, 50; friendships in, 51, 53–54, 57, 58; guidelines for new teachers in, 53; induction days in, 54–55, 55, 57, 66; Jesus Christ as role model for, 49, 50, 53, 58, 65; matching mentors and mentees in, 51–54, 58–59; as mission and ministry, 49, 50, 54, 66; PLCs in, 56, 58; principal and teacher differences in, 59; principal monthly meetings as, 59–60; by principals, 50; of principals, 58–66; program of, 49–50; as spiritual, pedagogical and professional, 49, 56, 57, 60; of teachers, 51–58; teaching and leadership qualities in, 50–51; unique differences of, 51
Cato Institute, 156
CFAs. *See* common formative assessments
CFGs. *See* Critical Friends Groups
Chao, G. T., 24
Chávez, Anna Maria, 153–154
Cheng, L., 19
Christian education. *See* Catholic school mentoring
Chun, J. U., 121–122
Clinton, Hillary Rodham, 151
collaboration, of universities and school districts, 43–44, 44, 46
collaborative mentoring, 7; in academic mentoring, 115, 124–125; boundaries, 115; CFGs as, 87, 96, 103–106; elements of, 93–94; lesson study model of, 87, 96, 99–103; models of, 95–107; as most effective, 115; PLCs for, 87, 93, 96, 96–99; principal's role in, 108–109; school reform based on, 86–88, 95, 106–107, 109; as school reform's missing link, 91–92; as social capital, 91–92; student achievement scores linked to, 91–92, 93–94; transformational leaders and, 120–121
collegiality, 71–72
comfort, in e-mentoring, 132–133
Common Core, 45, 86, 97, 99, 141
common formative assessments (CFAs), 97–99
communication: in assistant professor mentoring, 69, 70, 78; in e-mentoring, 131–132, 142; language barriers in, 18; language bias in, 153–154, 160; male

compared to female, 159–160, 161; morality in, 159
community, in e-mentoring, 136–137, 139–140
community of learners, 63, 65, 66, 67
Connors, R., 90–91
contemporary approaches, to mentoring, 7–8
contemporary literacies, 135–136
Contreras-McGavin, M., 118
Cooper, Bruce S., viii
"Co-Opt the Old Boys' Club: Make It Work for Women" (Lang), 156
Copeland, S., 150
coping and copying, x
Covey, Stephen, 54, 78–79
Critical Friends Groups (CFGs): defined, 104; as learning focused, 104; as PLC, 104; principals determining success of, 106; protocols of, 105; studies regarding, 105–106; as teacher collaboration model, 87, 96, 103–106
Crocker, C., 40–41
Crowson, R., 119
Csikszentmihalyi, M., 113–114
culture clashes, in e-mentoring, 138–139
cultures of accountability, 90–91, 95–96, 103

Dana, J. A., 151
Daresh, 41
Darling-Hammond, Linda, 134
Davis, J., 117
Deal, T., 93
Derrida, Jacques, 158–160
developmental processes, 5, 10; phases of, 5; redefining relationship in, 5, 10
discrimination. *See* gender bias
doctoral students. *See* international graduate and doctoral students
do-it-yourself e-mentoring, 143–144
Dougherty, T. W., 3–4
DuFour, R., 95, 96, 97, 108
Dukess, L. F., 122
Dunne, F., 106

Eaker, R., 96
Eby, L., 24

educators, vii. *See also* faculty; principals; teachers
Ehrich, L. C., 157
Ellerson, N. M., 149
e-mentoring, 7; access increased by, 130–131; assessments as ongoing in, 133–134; best practices for implementing, 140–142; blogging in, 129, 135, 140, 141, 143; comfort of, 132–133; communication in, 131–132, 142; community in, 136–137; contemporary literacies in, 135–136; culture clashes in, 138–139; defined, 129; do-it-yourself, 143–144; efficacy of, 144–145; goals, time expectations and assessments in, 140–141; as informal mentoring, 142, 143–144; as instant, 129, 131–132; local knowledge loss in, 138; matching mentees and mentors, 142, 143–144; millennial culture in, 129, 132, 138–139, 142; multimedia engagement of, 134–135; online community maintenance in, 139–140; personalization of, 133; program design of, as untested, 130, 137–138; promises of, 130–137; recruiting and preparing mentors for, 141–142; reflective thinking in, 135–136, 140, 143; relationships in, 136–137; resources for, 143–144; self-mentoring by, 143–144; shadowing and observing in, 139; teacher retention by, 129, 131, 138, 144–145; technology in, 137–140, 141, 145; time issues in, 140
emotional intelligence, 116
engagement, 106, 134–135
Erickson, Donald A., viii
ethical behavior, 123
evaluations: peer mentoring for teacher, 89; by principals, 86, 89, 108–109; of principal's mentoring, 40, 44, 45; test scores linked to teacher, 86, 88–89
Evans, H., 90
expertise, development process of, 135–136
exposure and opportunities, for mentees, 75–76

faculty: role of, 70, 124–125. *See also* assistant professors, mentoring of; international graduate and doctoral students
female: communication, 159–160, 161; leadership styles, 157; mentors for women, 150
Fernanadez, 86
Fisher, J. L., 120
focus, 74
formal mentoring, 80; informal compared to, 3–4; problems with, 80–81
formative assessments, 97–98
Free and Freedom Schools: A National Survey (Cooper), viii, ix
friends. *See* Critical Friends Groups (CFGs)
friendships, 51, 53–54, 57, 58, 74, 76
Fullan, M., 36–37, 41–42, 78–79, 93, 95

Gall, 106
Gardner, P. D., 24
Gawande, A., 135
gender bias, 152–153, 157–160, 160
gendering of organizations, 157
gender roles, and women leaders, 154–160
Gilligan, Carol, 158–160, 161
Ginsberg, R., 38
glass ceiling, 151–152, 156
goal establishment, in e-mentoring, 140–141
Godshalk, V. M., 122–123
Goldring, E., 119
Goldstein, H., 121
Goleman, D., 116
Goodboy, A., 123
Good Mentoring (Nakamura and Shernoff), 24
graduate students. *See* international graduate and doctoral students
Grogan, M., 149–150
Grumet, M. R., 80
guidelines, for mentoring, 39, 39–40, 40, 53

Haberkorn, J. T., 123
Haggard, D. L., 3–4
Hammond, Jan, x
Harris, S., 40–41

Hartman, K., 37–38
Hecht, U. S., 122
Heller, D., 107
Hess, A., 156
Hickman, 90–91
Hiebert, J., 86
Hiemstra, R., 21
higher education mentoring. *See* academic mentoring
history, of mentoring, 2–4
Hoff, D. L., 152
honesty, 72–73, 78, 80
Hooker, C., 113–114
hope and help, x
Horng, E., 155
Howarth, M., 119
Huang, T., 78
Huntley, H., 18

In a Different Voice (Gilligan), 158–159
individual responsibility, for success, 157–158, 160
induction days, 54–55, 55, 57, 66
informal mentoring, 71, 80; benefits of, 81; e-mentoring as, 142, 143–144; formal compared to, 3–4; shadowing and observing as, 139
instant mentoring. *See* e-mentoring
institutional perspectives, 17–18
international graduate and doctoral students: academic expectations and, 15–16; faculty's mentoring role in, 17, 20, 25, 26–29, 29; increase in, 13, 14, 17; institutional perspective of, 17–18; issues of, 16–17, 18–20, 25; language barriers of, 18; mentoring model for, 26–29; mentoring specific to, 23–26; needs of, 13, 14, 17, 18–20, 23; SDL for, 20–22, 26–28, 27, 28, 29; social support networks for, 19; students' perspective of, 18–20, 25–26; theoretical foundations for mentoring models for, 20–29, 26; TL for, 20, 22–23, 26, 27, 28, 29; transition issues for, 16, 23, 26, 28–29
internships, 41, 44, 45–46

Jesus Christ, 49, 50, 53, 58, 65

Kaczmarek, J., 20
Kezar, A., 118
Kim, Y., 157–158
Knowles, M. S., 21
Kowalski, T. J., 9, 149
Kram, K. E., 3, 5, 7, 8–9
Ku, H. K., 18, 19, 25–26

LaForrest, L., 151–152
Laird, D., 119
Lang, Ilene, 156
language: barriers, 18; bias, 153–154, 160
Law, B., 95
leadership: in academic mentoring, 114–115; academic mentoring roles in, 117–118; androgynous, 154–155; benefits of, 119–122; caring communities created by, 95; of Catholic school principals, 61; Catholic school qualities of, 50–51; challenges of, 38; collaborative mentoring for effective, 115, 124–125; complexity of, 36, 39, 42; components of productive, 41–42; components of successful mentoring program for, 40–41; effective, 122–123; emotional intelligence of, 116; internship criteria for, 41, 44, 45–46; learning leaders as, 108; male and female styles of, 154–155, 157; mentoring as, 114; mentoring guidelines needed for, 39, 39–40, 40; mentoring in future, 44–46; preparing for, 43–44; principals and teachers sharing of, 91; principal's role in, 42–43; reasons for poor mentoring in, 39–40; self-management in, 116, 124; service-oriented, 65–66; successful, 36–37; training for, 37–38, 39–40; transcendental, 65; transformational, 118–119, 119–121, 121–122, 122–123; university and school district collaboration for, 43–44, 44, 46. *See also* women leaders
leadership applications, 8–10
Leana, C. R., 91–92
Lean In: Women, Work, and the Will to Lead (Sandberg), 153
learning focused teaching: CFGs for, 104; lesson study model for, 100–101; PLCs as, 96–99; for school reform, 109
learning leaders, 108
lesson study model: as collaborative mentoring, 87, 96, 99–103; as learning focused, 100–101; for student achievement, 99–103, 106
Levinson, D. J., 2–3
Lewis, A., 106
Li, C., 20
Little, J. W., 93–94
local knowledge, 138
Loeb, S., 155
"Looking Back to Look Forward: Revisiting in a Different Voice" (Gilligan), 159–160, 161
Lovely, S., 44
Luebeck, J., 130–131, 132

Mahar, R., 37–38
male: communication, 159–160, 161; leadership styles, 157; mentors for women, 150
"Management of Gender Roles: Marketing the Androgynous Leadership Style in the Classroom and General Workplace" (Way and Marques), 154–155
M.A.R.C.H., defined, vii–x
Marques, J., 154–155
Marsicano, Hazel, 151
Marzano, R., 108
matching, mentors and mentees: by approaches to mentoring, 4, 10; in Catholic schools, 51–54, 58–59; in e-mentoring, 142, 143–144
McCaffery, P., 117
McCord, R. S., 149
McCray, C. M., 78
McCray, C. R., 80
McCrea, N. L., 157
McElroy, Neil H., viii
McFadden, Cynthia, 153–154
McLaughlin, M. W., 94
mentees, 4; matching, with mentors, 4, 10, 51–54, 58–59, 142, 143–144; mentor relationship with, 6–7; opportunities and exposure for, 75–76
Mentor (character), 2, 70
mentoring: approaches to, 4–8, 10; defined, 1, 3–4, 69, 69–70, 113; formal,

3–4, 80, 80–81; functions of, 4; history of, 2–4; informal, 3–4, 71, 80, 81, 139, 142, 143–144; and leadership, 35–36, 39, 39–40, 40, 44–46, 114; personal reflections on, 71–77, 80–81; phases of, 5; reasons for poor, 39–40; as relationship based, 113–114, 118; value of, 1, 1–2, 3–4, 8–9, 24–25; of women leaders, 150–151, 160. *See also* academic mentoring; Catholic School mentoring; collaborative mentoring; e-mentoring; international graduate and doctoral students; peer mentoring

Mentoring at Work: Developmental Relationships in Organizational Life (Kram), 3, 7, 8–9

The Mentor: Leading with Heart (Hammond and Senor), x

mentors: accountability of, 39, 43, 44; defined, 3–4, 24; finding, 9–10, 10, 71; matching, with mentees, 4, 10, 51–54, 58–59, 142, 143–144; mentee relationship with, 6–7; qualities of effective, 7, 114–115

Mezirow, J., 21, 22
Middlebrooks, A. E., 123
millennial culture, 129, 132, 138–139, 142
Mills, R., 37–38
Miner, B., 89
mission: Catholic school principals as driven by, 60–61, 66; of Catholic schools, 49, 50, 54, 66
Mitchell, S. N., 152
modeling with meaning, viii–ix
moral imperative, of school reform, 87, 95, 106, 107, 109
morality, in communication, 159
Moran, W., 120
multimedia engagement, in e-mentoring, 134–135
Myles, J., 19
Myung, J., 155

Nakamura, J., 24, 113–114
National Foundation for the Improvement of Education (NFIE), 7
National School Reform Faculty (NSRF), 89, 103–104, 105
Nave, B., 106

NCLB. *See* No Child Left Behind Act
New Girl Order: Are Men in Decline? (Cato Institute), 156
NFIE. *See* National Foundation for the Improvement of Education
No Child Left Behind Act (NCLB), 88
Northouse, P. G., 117
NSRF. *See* National School Reform Faculty

Obama, Barack, 88
Obiakor, F. E., 80
observing and shadowing, 139
The Odyssey, 2, 70
old boys' club, 155–156
Olivas, M., 20
online community, in e-mentoring, 139–140
opportunities and exposure, for mentees, 75–76
organic mentoring. *See* informal mentoring
organizational theory, of school reform, 90
orientation: for Catholic school principals, 61–63; induction days as, 54–55, 55, 57, 66
Orpen, C., 122

pedagogical mentoring, in Catholic schools, 49, 56, 57, 60
peer mentoring, 8; for school reform, 85; as superficial fad, 86; superficial implementation of, 86; for teacher evaluations, 89; teacher retention by, 89; of teachers, 85
Peplau, L. A., 117
Perrewe, P., 123
personal connections, 76–77
personalization, of e-mentoring, 133
Petersen, G. J., 149
Peterson, K. D., 93
phases, of mentoring, 5
Pirouznia, M., 157
PLCs. *See* professional learning communities
Plenary Representatives, 73
Pogodzinski, B., 142
political savvy, 74
Pounder, J., 123

President's Commission on School Finance, viii, ix
principals: CFG success dependent on, 106; collaborative mentoring guided by, 108–109; criteria for successful, 36–37; evaluating mentoring of, 40, 44, 45; gender bias among, 152; leadership shared with teachers by, 91; as learning leaders, 108; role of, 42–43, 58–59; teacher evaluations by, 86, 89, 108–109
principals, of Catholic schools: Catholic School Leadership Program for, 60–61, 63–64; community of learners for, 63, 65, 66, 67; leadership principles of, 61; mentoring by, 50; mentoring of, 58–66; mission-driven leadership in, 60–61, 66; mission of, 61; monthly meetings for, 59–60; orientation week for, 61–63; service-oriented leadership of, 65–66; survival guide for, 61–63; teacher mentoring different than, 59; transcendental leadership of, 65
privilege, 158, 159
professional development, of teachers, 56
professional learning communities (PLCs): in Catholic schools, 56, 58; CFAs in, 97–99; CFG as, 104; as collaborative mentoring, 87, 93, 96, 96–99; features of, 96; as learning focused, 96–99; process summary of, 98–99; for student achievement, 96–99, 103, 106
professional mentoring, in Catholic schools, 49, 56, 57, 60
program design: in Catholic school mentoring, 49–50; in e-mentoring, 130, 137–138
promises, of e-mentoring, 130–137
protégés. *See* mentee
publication assistance, viii–ix, ix, 24, 25, 71, 76–77

Rafferty, A., 119
Ravitch, D., 88–89
recruiting e-mentors, 141–142
Reeves, D. B., 86–87
reflections, on mentoring, 71–77, 80–81
reflective thinking, in e-mentoring, 135–136, 140, 143
reform. *See* school reform

relationships, 69, 70, 78–79, 81; attachment theory of, 6; barriers to, 6, 10; collaborative mentoring, 115, 124–125; developmental process for redefining, 5, 10; in e-mentoring, 136–137; in informal mentoring, 81; mentor and mentee, 6–7; mentoring based on, 113–114, 118
resources, for e-mentoring, 143–144
retention, of teachers: e-mentoring for, 129, 131, 138, 144–145; peer mentoring for, 89
review and revise, ix–x
Rice, Condoleezza, 153
"Role of Mentors in Developing Careers: Do Women Need Mentors?" (Marsicano), 151
Root, R. L., 158

Sandberg, Sheryl, 153–154
Scandura, T. A., 122
Schlossberg, N. K., 28–29
school district and university collaboration, 43–44, 44, 46
school reform: accountability culture for, 90–91, 95–96, 103; caring communities for, 95; CFGs for, 87, 96, 103–106; learning focused teaching for, 109; moral imperative in, 87, 95, 106, 107, 109; organizational theory of, 90; peer mentoring for, 85; shared leadership for, 91, 94; superficial implementations of, 86–87; teacher collaboration as missing link in, 91–92; teacher collaboration for, 86–88, 95, 106–107, 109; teachers as driving force for, 86; theoretical background for, 90–95
Schuman, L. A., 122
SDL. *See* self-directed learning
Sears, D. O., 117
Seasons of a Man's Life (Levinson), 2–3
self-directed learning (SDL), 20–22, 26–28, 27, 28, 29
self-management, 116, 124
self-mentoring, 143–144
Senge, 36
Senor, Rita, x
Sergiovanni, 95
service-oriented leadership, 65–66

Seven Habits of Highly Effective People (Covey), 54
shadowing and observing, 139
Shakeshaft, C., 149–150
Shannon, A., 116
Shernoff, D. J., 24, 113–114
Sieverdes, C. M., 122
Simonsen, L., 130–131, 132
Slattery, P., 157
Smith, T., 90–91
social capital, 91–92
social support networks, 19
Sosik, J. J., 121–122, 122–123
spiritual mentoring, 49, 56, 57, 60
Starratt, R. J., 79
Stepanek, J., 103
stereotypes. *See* gender bias
Stigler, J., 86
St. Mary's School. *See* Catholic school mentoring
Stogdill, R. M., 117
Strouse, S. K., 122
student achievement: CFAs for measuring, 97–99; CFGs for improving, 103–106; collaborative mentoring linked to, 91–92, 93–94; lesson study model for, 99–103, 106; PLCs for improving, 96–99, 103, 106; teachers' social capital linked to, 91–92
students. *See* international graduate and doctoral students
Suanmali, C., 21
superintendents, 8; gender bias among, 152; women, 149, 150
support: for assistant professors, 71–72; guidelines for new teacher, 53; social networks of, 19
survival guide, for Catholic school principals, 61–63

Talbert, J. E., 94
Taylor, S. E., 117
teachers: accountability of, 85, 86; Catholic school qualities of, 50–51; in Catholic schools, 51–58; CFGs for, 87, 96, 103–106; collaboration as missing link for, 91–92; collaboration by, for school reform, 86–88, 95; evaluations of, 86, 88–89, 108–109; first year mentoring calendar for, 55–56; induction days for new, 54–55, 55, 57, 66; modeling by, viii–ix; peer mentoring for, 85; post-first year mentoring of, 58; principal mentoring different than, 59; principals sharing leadership with, 91; professional development for, 56; retention of, 89, 129, 131, 138, 144–145; school reform driven by, 86; social capital of, 91–92; support guidelines for new, 53; teamwork among, 85, 86; unique needs of individual, 57
teamwork, 85, 86. *See also* collaborative mentoring; peer mentoring
technology, in e-mentoring, 137–140, 141, 145
test scores: in NCLB, 88; for school reform, 88–89; teacher evaluations based on, 86, 88–89
Thurer, S. L., 160
time, for e-mentoring, 140, 140–141
TL. *See* transformative learning
training, for school leadership, 37–38, 39–40
transcendental leadership, 65
transformational leadership, 118–119, 119–121, 121–122, 122–123
transformative learning (TL), 20, 22–23, 26, 27, 28, 29
transition issues, 16, 23, 26, 28–29
Turban, D. B., 3–4

university and school district collaboration, 43–44, 44, 46
University Council of Education Administration, 72

Villar, A., 144
voice, of women, 158–160, 161

The Wallace Foundation, 39
Walz, P., 24
Wang, S., 6
Washington, C. E., 150–151
Way, A. D., 154–155
Web 2.0 tools, 143–144
Wiburg, K., 86, 87, 99, 103
Wilbanks, J. E., 3–4

Williams, E. A., 122
Wilmore, E. L., 46
Wilson-Jones, L., 151–152
Women in the Superintendency: Discarded Leadership (Dana and Bourisaw), 151–152
women leaders: in administration, 149–150; androgynous leadership for, 154–155; Ban Bossy campaign for, 153–154; female compared to male mentors for, 150; gender bias limiting, 152–153, 157, 160; gender roles and, 154–160; glass ceiling for, 151–152, 156; individual responsibility for success of, 157–158, 160; mentoring for success of, 150–151, 160; old boys' club and, 155–156; as superintendents, 149, 150; women's "voice" in, 158–160, 161

Yawn, C. D., 80
Yoon, S. A., 132
Yoshida, 86, 99
Young, P., 149
Yun, N. Y., 121–122

About the Contributors

Karen Andronico currently serves as an instructional assistant principal in a diversely populated New York City high school where she supervises English, performing and visual arts, foreign language, and ESL teachers. She also prepares aspiring teachers to meet the challenges of the teaching profession as an adjunct associate professor at the College of New Rochelle. She earned a doctorate in educational leadership from Fordham University in 2013 and has since published an article in collaboration with Dr. Bruce S. Cooper in *JEPPA*, an online educational journal.

Dr. Floyd D. Beachum is the Bennett Professor of Urban School Leadership at Lehigh University, where he is also an associate professor and program director for educational leadership in the College of Education. He received his doctorate in leadership studies from Bowling Green State University with an emphasis in educational administration. His research interests include: leadership in urban education, moral and ethical leadership, and social justice issues in K–12 schools.

Dr. Rhonda Bondie is assistant professor of special education at Fordham University. She was a teacher and administrator in public schools for more than twenty years. Rhonda's research focuses on instructional methods for academically diverse classrooms and teacher preparation using technology.

Deirdre Callahan is currently the assistant principal of Middle School 343/The Academy of Applied Mathematics and Technology in District 7, one of only twenty schools of the New York City Department of Education's 1,700 to receive six consecutive A ratings on their school's report card, three of them under her administration. Prior to working at MS 343, Ms. Callahan was the assistant principal of MS 319, one of only twelve schools to receive seven consecutive A ratings, three of them under her administration. She is a former Peace Corps volunteer, having served two and a half years as an English as a foreign language teacher and athletic coach on the tiny island of Temwen, Pohnpei, in the Federated States of Micronesia.

Bruce S. Cooper, PhD, is professor emeritus at Fordham University, Graduate School of Education, with a focus on research including: (1) politics and policy in education, with his books *Better Policies, Better Schools* and *Handbook of Education Politics and Policy*; (2) in private school religious education, with his book *Blurring the Lines* and "Finding a Golden Mean in Education Policy: Centering Religious and Public Schools" in the *Peabody Journal of Education*; and (3) fixing school problems, with his books *Fixing Truancy Now* with Jon Shute and *Truancy Revised* with Rita Brause.

Kenneth Cuthbert is a twenty-nine-year veteran of the New York City Department of Education, the nation's largest public school system. He has served as teacher in a school of more than three thousand students, as assistant principal in a specialized high school of more than five thousand students, lead principal of a multischool campus, turn-around principal of a struggling high school, transformation mentor principal, and as network mentor principal for a New York City network with multiple new principals. His work has been highlighted in the media and recognized by public officials.

Dr. Jan Hammond is associate professor at Long Island University in the Department of Educational Leadership and Administration and the CEIT Interdisciplinary Doctoral program. She is professor emerita and former chair in the Department of Educational Administration at the State University of New York at New Paltz. Dr. Hammond has held positions of middle and high school teacher, principal, and assistant superintendent for business. Her educational research expands to Europe, Japan, Singapore, and India. Her recent book, *The Mentor* (2014), highlights best theories and practices for school leaders. She is past president of New York State ASCD, CADEA, and NYSAWA, and a member of the NYSED Board of Regents Professional Standards and Practices Board.

Sr. Mary Ann Jacobs, SSC, is assistant professor in the School of Education and Health at Manhattan College in Riverdale, New York. She teaches pedagogy courses to preservice teachers at the undergraduate level in secondary education. She also teaches potential school leaders in the School Building Leadership Program. She may be contacted at maryann.jacobs@manhattan.edu.

Kathleen P. King, EdD, is professor of higher education and student affairs at University of South Florida in Tampa, Florida. Kathy's major areas of research and expertise include transformative learning, leadership, faculty development, distance learning, instructional technology, and diversity. The International Continuing and Adult Education Hall of Fame recognized Dr. King's outstanding contributions to adult and higher education with her 2011 induction. As an award-winning author who has published more than thirty books, she enjoys international travel, different cultures, and is a popular keynote speaker, mentor, and professor. You may reach "Kathy" via drkpking@gmail.com.

Julie Leos is a PhD student in the Higher Education Administration program at The University of South Florida. Julie works in the MUMA College of Business as an academic advisor and is also the coordinator of a Living Learning program for high achieving business students. Julie has worked in College Student Affairs for the past nine years. Her research interests include women's issues in higher education, workplace excellence, and the benefits of wellness on workplace engagement. Her email address is julieleos@usf.edu.

Michael R. Mascellino has been an educator and consultant for over eight years. He has also served as an analyst and program developer for several school departments over the course of his career. Michael's ideas on school leadership and educator development have been motivated by the need to better prepare our school leaders and teachers in an evolving skill-based market.

Dr. Carlos R. McCray is division chair and associate professor for the Educational Leadership, Administration, and Policy Division. He is co-author of the books *Cultural Collision and Collusion: Reflections on Hip-Hop Culture, Values*, and *Schools and School Leadership in a Diverse Society: Helping Schools Prepare All Students for Success*. Professor McCray has worked with school leaders and educators in the metropolitan areas of Atlanta, New York City, and London.

Lu Norstrand, MPhil, MA, is a PhD student of higher education administration at University of South Florida. She has earned both an MPhil from Nankai University in Tianjin, China, and an MA in adult education from the University of South Florida in Tampa. Lu's major areas of research include adult education, globalization and higher education, and leadership as well as Eastern and Western philosophical inquiry. Lu's email address: lubai@mail.usf.edu.

Richard Savior, EdD, is assistant professor of business, management, and economics at the State University of New York, Empire State College. He received his doctorate in educational leadership, administration, and policy from Fordham University, and his research is focused in executive leadership, organizational development, and globalization.

Heather Wynne, PhD, is a nationally certified school psychologist who has worked in schools, hospitals, and agencies throughout New York and Connecticut. She specializes in social-emotional interventions and positive behavioral support services. Her research focuses on educational practices and achievement motivation.

www.ingramcontent.com/pod-product-compliance
Lightning Source LLC
Chambersburg PA
CBHW030139240426
43672CB00005B/183